GLOWING PRAISE FOR THIS UPROARIOUSLY FUNNY RELATIONSHIP GUIDE

"For all its self-deprecating comedy, this volume provides valuable insight into typical relationship potholes, including chick-flick conflict, the dreaded 'Do I look fat?' conversation, and chronic miscommunication."

—*Publishers Weekly*

"Nonstop fun and a highly entertaining read . . . *Women Are Crazy, Men Are Stupid* makes a great gift for your favorite couple, and should be tucked away in everyone's book shelf for easy reference."

—*Sacramento Book Review*

"What I love most about this hilarious battle of the sexes book is that while you're laughing it morphs into a great love story."

—Debra Messing

"You'd be crazy not to buy this book for the man in your life. And if he won't read it, serve it with bacon."

—Tim Allen

"Morris and Lee are stupid and crazy so you don't have to be. The chapter on romance is a classic!"

—Gigi Levangie Grazer

"This book is laugh-out-loud funny. And I don't just mean that 'lol' stuff. I actually laughed out loud. The surprise is that a book this funny is also so wise. It's bursting with real insights and universal truths. At the same time, it's deeply personal. Howard and Jenny spare us no intimate details of their relationship."

—David Crane, co-creator of *Friends*

WOMEN ARE CRAZY, MEN ARE STUPID

THE SIMPLE TRUTH TO A COMPLICATED RELATIONSHIP

Howard J. Morris and Jenny Lee

New York   London   Toronto   Sydney

GALLERY BOOKS
A Division of Simon & Schuster, Inc.
1230 Avenue of the Americas
New York, NY 10020

First Gallery Books trade paperback edition August 2010

GALLERY BOOKS and colophon are trademarks of Simon & Schuster, Inc.

For information about special discounts for bulk purchases, please contact Simon & Schuster Special Sales at 1-866-506-1949 or business@simonandschuster.com.

The Simon & Schuster Speakers Bureau can bring authors to your live event. For more information or to book an event contact the Simon & Schuster Speakers Bureau at 866-248-3049 or visit our website at www.simonspeakers.com.

Designed by Dana Sloan

Manufactured in the United States of America

10   9   8   7   6   5   4   3   2   1

The hardcover edition was catalogued as follows by the Library of Congress:
Morris, Howard J.
     Women are crazy, men are stupid : the simple truth to a complicated relationship / by Howard J. Morris and Jenny Lee.
     p. cm.
  1. Man-woman relationships. I. Lee, Jenny. II. Title.
  HQ801.M777 2009
306.7—dc22
                                        2009004762

ISBN 978-1-4165-9505-2
ISBN 978-1-4165-9541-0 (pbk)
ISBN 978-1-4391-0974-8 (ebook)

FOR MY MOM AND DAD, MURIEL AND
LARRY MORRIS, WITH ADMIRATION AND AWE
FOR THEIR FIRST FIFTY YEARS TOGETHER

—HOWARD

FOR MY MOM, HAEKYONG, AND MY
AWESOME BROTHER, JOHN, WITH MUCH LOVE.
AND, FOR EVERY CRAZY WOMAN WHO HAS
EVER LOVED A STUPID MAN

—JENNY

CONTENTS

INTRODUCTION

I did it again.

This time it happened so fast I didn't even realize it. I never saw it coming. I thought it was going to be a fairly uneventful night. No such luck. The look on her face was as unmistakable as it was recognizable: the astounded scowl. The shake of the head in complete and utter disbelief. The look that says, "Did you *really* just do the horrible thing that you just did to me? *Again!?*" And then her words explode in my face like machine gun fire: *"Is it that you don't love me enough? Or is it that your needs just always come first? Or is it that you're just too stupid to realize what I want?"*

"THESE ARE MY OPTIONS?" I scream. "THESE ARE MY ONLY OPTIONS?"

The answer is number three, of course. The answer is *always* three. I'm just too stupid. But she doesn't want to hear this. She thinks the fact that I'm a voracious reader and splendid conversationalist means that I should have a clue as to what she wants from me. But I don't. Most of the time I'm not really

1

sure what she's upset about or even what the hell she's talking about. Because frankly, while she's totally loving and wonderful most of the time, the rest of the time she seems crazier than a shithouse rat. (And I mean this with all due affection, hon.)

The heat of this particular moment eventually died down, but over and over again we'd inevitably find ourselves plopped on our couch, staring forlornly into space, she wondering how I could be such an unfathomable imbecile, and I, once again, trying to figure out how she could be such a big bowl of wacko. But then one night, she just shrugged, threw up her hands, and as something like acceptance or defeat seemed to wash over her, she said, "That's just it, isn't it? It's as simple as that."

"What is?" I asked.

"Women are crazy and men are stupid."

And suddenly all the lights in a dark world were turned on.

"Women are crazy. And men are stupid," she said again.

"Now *there's* your next book!" I exclaimed.

Jenny Lee, the person responsible for these brilliant words and my girlfriend, laughed off my suggestion, as authors are apt to do when someone says something to them like "Now *there's* your next book!" (And to be fair, she once told me she was having a lot of "misdirected, overagonizing emotions" and I thought that was a good title for her next book, too. So perhaps title spotting isn't one of my gifts.)

But the next day I found myself unable to shake this notion. The more I thought about it, the more it made me laugh and then nod knowingly to myself. But what was it that I knew? And how did I know that I knew it? Yet know it I did: *Women are crazy. Men are stupid.* It seemed like such a simple yet revelatory way of seeing things. I wondered if this could be the starting point from which to begin to understand the most important but vexing relationships in our lives.

I then mentioned the phrase to my friend Sean, a man often stumped by the actions of the fairer sex, and of his girlfriend in particular. Upon hearing these words, Sean laughed as I had and then did the *exact same nodding knowingly thing*. And I could see that the same lightbulb that had been turned on in my head was now on in his. He then spent the next three days telling his girlfriend that she was completely nuts and he was a total idiot. (They later broke up. I'm pretty sure it was due to more than just him doing that.)

The other reason this idea intrigued me so much was that in essence I've been living the subject of stupid men and crazy women my whole life. And in my work too. Much of my writing has been about clueless men and the insane women they're clueless about. I'd written a play about the unbelievable struggle for the sexes just to communicate with each other, called *Men Don't Share*. And my entire television career has been about men and women's inability to comprehend one another. Most notably, I was a writer for four years on *Home Improvement*, the insanely popular television show with Tim Allen. I also knew that at forty-four I was now smart enough to put some things together I never had before, while still being stupid enough to keep it real. By the end of the day I knew I had to write this book.

I also knew I was too stupid to write it myself.

I needed help from the funniest, most honest, and balls-out craziest woman I knew. The person who'd said those magical words in the first place. When I approached Jenny that night about working together with me on this book, she was intrigued by the idea but wary about the possible detrimental effects it might have on our relationship. But I was undeterred. "We'll do it *together*!" I enthused. "We'll be the couple who writes together!" And that appealed to the romantic in her. She thought it was a lot more exciting than being the couple who takes ballroom dancing together.

So the next day I stood by the door waiting for Jenny to come home from her job writing for the TV show *Samantha Who?* And I could barely wait to share my freshly penned insights with her. Her reaction to my introduction went fairly well. But the first chapter—the one I was calling "Am I Fat?"— was of more concern to her. She took one look at the title and asked me, "Is this what you really think? That I'm fat?"

I immediately wished we'd gone ballroom dancing. Step, glide, glide. Step, glide, glide . . .

JENNY: When my darling boyfriend, Howard, came to me and said that he thought we should write a book together I wasn't sure if he was joking or not (welcome to the world of two comedy writers living together). So I defaulted to what I hoped his answer would be, which is that of course he was joking. *Ha. Ha. Ha. Look at you, my funny guy. I mean, that's the craziest thing I've ever heard of, and who better to know crazy than me, get it? And not only is it the craziest thing I've ever heard of, but it's also downright stuu—oh shit—pid,* which is when I knew he wasn't joking.

He was serious, so much so that he had already written the introduction to a book that wasn't even written yet, as well as chapter 1, which was entitled "Am I Fat?" (Later retitled at gunpoint.) Now before I could even begin to wax poetic on the insanity of this endeavor, I found myself first tackling the more important task, which was to find out who exactly was this "Am I Fat?" person in question—you know, the person that he was referencing—because I knew, or rather I prayed to god for his sake, that Howard, my love, knew better than to write about me when it came to this particular topic. Because as everyone in the world knows, even the stupid ones, nothing makes a woman go from zero to crazy faster than the topic of her weight.

His first indicator that crazy had come a-knockin' was the tone of my voice when I said, "So, uh, who did you write about in chapter one? Hmmm?" The second and more leading indicator was that I wouldn't even let him answer the question I'd just asked him. "I'm just wondering because I *know* you would never write about me when it comes to said topic, right?"

There were five full seconds of us blinking at each other with no one speaking before we both lunged for the chapter that was lying between us on the dining room table. Tie. We each had a grip from either side, and unfortunately, I had it upside down, so I had a hard time scanning the first page, which to be fair did not have my name on it. But given his white knuckles and the bead of sweat that was now traveling south on his forehead, I knew the answer.

"Are you insane?" I asked.

Through gritted teeth he responded, "Isn't that your department?"

Not funny. With one big heave-ho (and maybe I yelled out, "Spider on your head!") I managed to get the pages away from him and I took off upstairs. He followed in hot pursuit, shouting at me, "See, this is what I mean. You're acting crazy.

Come on, we're comedy writers! We exaggerate for the sake of the funny! It's our job. We have to eat."

I shouted back, *"I'm a fat woman, don't you think I know we have to eat?!"*

HOWARD: That's when I realized: *Hey, wait a minute. She's acting totally crazy. She's now being the crazy woman that this book is about. It's the book in action! It's living proof of the premise! This is great! Except for one thing. If she's acting crazy, me acting stupid can't be far behind. It's like a cause and effect. But I've always maintained that she's the cause and I'm just the effect.*

JENNY: I stormed back down the stairs, having found the damning evidence in the middle of page two: "So this morning when she glanced in the mirror, inspecting her tummy . . ." EEGADS, this wasn't stupid; this was suicide. "Inspecting my tummy? Really? Inspecting my tummy." (He winced again; sarcastic repetition on my part meant there would be no mercy.) "Wow, so interesting that I would be inspecting my tummy when this morning you insisted that I didn't even *have* a tummy." I shrieked, "I knew it! You think I'm fat!"

"I don't think you're fat. I think you're beautiful."

Was he kidding me? Did he actually think that buttering me up with the ol' "you're beautiful" line was going to save his sorry ass? Didn't he know that I was holding all the proof I needed in my hands before him? I shook the pages in his face just in case he had forgotten. "You [shake] do [shake] too [shake] think [shake] I'm [shake] fat. It's right here in black and white. Are you calling me a liar too?"

Suddenly, he gave me his most adorable smile. "See? Look how crazy you are right now, cupcake."

HOWARD: Let's just say I found out it's never a good idea to call a woman "cupcake" while on the subject of her weight. But it was now more clear than ever how qualified we were to write this book. And let's face it, a lot of books about relationships have self-proclaimed "experts" with suspect, if any, credentials in their chosen field. Even memoirs by drug addicts aren't real! But I'm not one of these slick smart guys tossing off pearls of wisdom from high atop Mount Evolved. No, I'm the real deal. I'm an incredibly dumb man. A genuine dunce. I have years and years of stupidity with women under my belt from which to draw knowledge. And I have witnesses. Women all across this nation ready to blurb this book attesting to my idiocy.

And no one is more qualified to talk about "crazy" than Jenny. I mean, she's such a major nut bag that— Uh, you know, on second thought, I probably shouldn't brag about my girlfriend. I could go on and on about her but I don't want to gush.

JENNY: "This book is a bad idea, like big time." Sometimes it's best to just say it plain and simple. I explained that his realization (in the unfortunately titled chapter "Am I Fat?") that a man should never engage in the "Am I fat?" debate with a woman was pretty smart for a big dummy. But to then *write about* his allegedly fat girlfriend was beyond stupid, because by doing so he was in fact *engaging* a woman (me) in the "Am I fat?" discussion, which he supposedly realized he should never do. Plus, he was proposing that he *continue* writing about all the stupid things that he does to make me crazy. How is that not going to annoy the crap out of me?

HOWARD: But this book is not about finger pointing, I explained. It's about coming out of denial that we're not these stupid, insane people and understanding how we all got so stupid and crazy in the first place. And what we can do about it now, if we're able to recognize who we really are and shine a light on some of our less deft moments in relationships. I mean, if one man could be even a *little* less stupid and one woman a *little* less crazy from reading this book, wouldn't that be an amazing thing?

JENNY: It's not that I didn't believe the title of the book to be true. (As I was the one who said it in the first place.) But I calmly explained that, sure, we could write a very funny book about men being stupid and women being crazy that could actually help couples communicate better, and we certainly could use our own relationship as fodder for this hilarious and insightful book. And I even acquiesced that hands down, there were probably no two people better suited than us to write such a book, seeing that we were just stupid and crazy enough to do it, *but that was my whole point.*

"Whuh?"

(This is the quintessential noise a stupid man makes when he doesn't understand a crazy woman. It's a combination of "What?" and "Huh?") Of course I knew why he was confused: What I *seemed* to be saying was that we should write this book together. But of course he was too stupid to understand that what I was *really* saying was the complete opposite of what I'd just said.

HOWARD: Whuh?

JENNY: He kept telling me that the beauty of the book was that it wasn't one-sided, and that America wanted—no, America *deserved* to know that the only thing that equaled the dizzying heights of his own stupidity was that his girlfriend was "crazier than a shithouse rat." OHMYGOD! What was he doing? I wailed, "What man is stupid enough to call his girlfriend that when speaking to his *actual* girlfriend? You're doing it AGAIN!"

"Again? I don't know what I did the first time! And it's not like I called you a shithouse rat outright, it was merely a metaphor for your craziness!"

This is when I interrupted him, speaking in a tone of voice like that of a woman whose straitjacket isn't securely tied—a little raspy and a lotta scary. "I know what a metaphor is."

HOWARD: She did look scary. Her eyes grew cold and dark and beady and whatever's smaller than beady.

JENNY: Then I dropped the bomb. "This book will break us up."

"We're not going to break up over the book," he pooh-poohed.

Wow, who died and made him king of the future?

"How can you say that? You don't know what's going to happen."

"And neither do you!"

He then did that thing where he takes off his glasses and rubs his face. This can either be read that he's tired or that he's trying to make sure that his eyeballs are secure in his head so they don't pop out as I go on.

HOWARD: "This book is not going to break us up!" I yelled again.

Unless it does. Then I'm stupid. And alone. I'm a lonely stupid man wishing I had me some crazy.

JENNY: "Fine, fine," I said in the way women for centuries have been saying "fine" when we really mean "not fine." "Even if the book doesn't break us up—and it will—how are we going to write it? How are crazy and stupid going to work together? Especially on a book about how crazy and stupid they are?!"

"But the book isn't *just about us,*" he shot back. "It's about everyone!"

"You keep saying that, but every time you sit down to write it's all about you being a moron and me being fat!"

"But that's America!"

"So I *am* fat?!"

"NOOOO!"

HOWARD: At this point a smarter man would have just abandoned ship. But one of the best things about my stupidity has always been the blind determination that comes along with it. I explained that since what I'd written had already upset her so much, I would write half the book and she would write the other half. "And we won't read each other's work! That way we're free to write how we really feel without fear of hurting each other. And we can then produce a book that will be more honest, more insightful, and more truthful."

"And how are we going to manage to write a book and not read it?" she asked.

"It's not like we won't read our own sections!" I explained. "And we'll just write an author's note on the first page. 'Note to reader: The authors of this book have not actually read it. And please don't tell them what's in it.'"

There was a pause as even I tried to comprehend what I'd just said.

Then we both sank into the couch in our usual dispirited positions, both staring into the wall for answers that never seemed to come. Finally I turned to her and said, "You really think writing this book could break us up?"

"It's a very real possibility," she said sadly. "I mean, it's not like a relationship isn't hard enough when you're just in *denial* about everything. But to actually bring stuff into the open and *write about it*—"

JENNY: Then Howard stopped me and pulled me into his arms. I was on the verge of tears and refused to look up at him. Stalemate. A perfect example of crazy locking horns with stupid. There we were, two people who loved each other and greatly respected each other's intelligence and sense of humor unable to find common ground. He threw his hands up in the air. "Okay. Forget the book. You are more important than any stupid book." He said it begrudgingly but I do think sincerely.

"Really?" Always a good idea to confirm.

He shrugged. "Yes, really."

I hugged him and he hugged me back. I kissed him and he kissed me back. Yay. I was happy. "I think we should write the book together."

There was a long silence and then he said what I knew he would.

"Whuh?"

In the end, we opted for a format in which Howard writes a chapter and then Jenny writes a response to it. (Except for chapter 4, which takes on the epic stupid/crazy subject of romance and Jenny just couldn't wait to respond so she jumped in much earlier.) The book is not so much a "he said/she said" as it is a "he says/she reacts." And yes, we both have read the whole book. It's really good! Turn the page!

1

THE HISTORY OF CRAZY AND STUPID

WHICH CAME FIRST? THE CRAZY OR THE STUPID?

The main reason women are crazy is that men are stupid.

—GEORGE CARLIN

No doubt exists that all women are crazy; it's only a question of degree.

—W. C. FIELDS

I drove a woman to an ashram once.

And when I say "drove" I don't mean in a car. And when I say "ashram" I do mean one of those places where you renounce sex and all your worldly possessions and chant "om shanti om" all day.

I drove her to an ashram. Where she lived for a good many years.

According to her I drove her crazy.

And when she says "drove her crazy" she doesn't mean that she was French, we made love by the Seine, and she squealed, "Oooh la la, monsieur! *You drive me craaaazeee!*" She means it more like "Hello? Insane asylum? Have a padded room and a straitjacket ready. I'll be there by three."

And she wasn't French.

Whether it was really me that drove her crazy or whether she was prone to crazy to begin with is a question we spent a lot of time debating. Perhaps it was just an unfortunate combination of the two. But as my friend Stephen said to me at the time, "I'm gonna give you a bye on this one. But if your next girlfriend ends up moving to an ashram, *I'm gonna know it's you.*" Well, I'm happy to note that none of my subsequent girlfriends (or one ex-wife) have moved to an ashram. At least not yet. But in an informal survey of these women one consistent theme emerges: my stupidity. And when they say "stupidity" it's not my lack of knowledge of state capitals that they're referring to, but more a kind of cluelessness they felt I showed in *dealing with them*. And their needs. In the end, they maintain it was my stupidity that drove them crazy. Which is interesting, because I always felt that it was their craziness that drove me stupid.

But that's just the problem, isn't it? So what's the answer?

Which came first, the crazy or the stupid?

It's the million-dollar question we all want the answer to. Are women crazy because men are stupid? Or are men stupid because women are crazy? Not surprisingly, the way we answer these two questions divides us quite neatly along gender lines. Because let's face it, we all have a lot invested in the answer. Women maintain that over the course of their lives they are driven slowly and methodically crazy by stupid men. And men maintain that it's impossible for any man to act smartly with a woman who's out of her freaking mind. If we can just prove one came first, the other side will have blaming rights for all eternity.

If only it were that simple.

Yes, there *is* an answer to which came first, the stupid or the crazy.

And the answer is here.

But I warn you, it offers only cold comfort to all you potential gleeful blamers. As in chemistry, every action causes a reaction, which in turn causes another reaction. Stupid causes crazy, which causes more stupid, which then results in more crazy, and so on. Only by going back and tracing the tortured and confused history of men acting stupid and women acting crazy from its very beginnings can we begin to fully understand the origins of insanity in the age of stupidity. Or the origins of stupidity in the age of insanity.

And as for blaming rights, don't worry, there's plenty to go around.

THE MYSTERY SOLVED

The history of men acting stupid is a long and varied one that always ends up with some idiot starting another war. But modern male stupidity as it applies specifically to women is far more interesting and relevant to our purposes. It actually has its roots in the playgrounds of our youth. It was there that we first became aware of girls. It was also there that we first realized that we liked these strange creatures. They made us feel funny. But *good* funny. A kind of warm and gushy funny. Of course in those early years it wasn't acceptable to talk about these new feelings with our peers for fear we'd get rightly harangued about the dangers of cooties. But still, we wanted this five-year-old ponytailed goddess to know that we had a thing for her. So what did we do?

We hit her.

Or pushed her into the mud and laughed at her. (I'm so sorry, Susan Freyberg.)

And here our stupidity begins.

But how could it be any other way? We never had a chance. The hit and the shove (and once again, I apologize, Susie) were the only ways we knew to express ourselves! They were our way of saying, "Hey, I know it's not cool for us to be hanging out 'cause of the whole cooties thing, but I dig you." And that blows up in our faces. She starts crying and we're completely unprepared for that. And she keeps crying until some adult explains to her that we hit her because we like her.

And here her craziness begins.

"Wait a minute. He shoves me into a mud puddle because he likes me? What is he? A five-year-old imbecile? My hamster is smarter than him!"

We're then beckoned into a lifetime of stupidity by some "well-meaning" adult who tells us not to hit but to "use our words." And here the wheels start to come off an already wobbly go-kart. Words are hard enough for grown men, let alone little boys. But still, we come up with a way to express ourselves. Because we just have to be around this fascinating but vexing softer creature. So we start to joke around with her. Like we do with our buddies. And it makes complete sense to us because *jokes are words*. And jokes are fun! And who doesn't like to have fun?!

Apparently, little girls.

Who, once again, run from the room hysterical, in tears, because they think we're making fun of them. And we are! *But only because we like them!* This is once again explained to the five-year-old ponytailed goddess (see? it was because I liked you, Cindy Cirello), who once again wonders at her own sanity. *"Okay, first the idiot punches me because he likes me. And now he's calling me names because he likes me? What does a boy do when he DOESN'T like you? AND HOW WILL I EVER BE ABLE TO TELL THE DIFFERENCE?!"*

An inauspicious beginning to be sure.

So now, with mistrust, uncertainty, and confusion abounding—all before puberty even sets in—both sexes limp back to their respective corners and spend the next few years in relative seclusion from each other. As the seasons of elementary school turn, we stealthily watch the "other" and study their every move.

And boy, do they move differently from us.

We live amongst them but we are not *of* them. (Kind of like Jane Goodall and the apes.) We observe our parents' relationship hoping to glean a tip or two about the whole sexual divide thing. (More often than not Mom and Dad are an advertisement for what *not* to do.) We watch television, and that's an even worse distortion of intergender relationships.

But then something happens.

Magically, certain things start to sink in. We learn that boy humor is different from girl humor. We also begin to understand the finer points of conversation. Or at least the basics.

It becomes clear that asking a girl about herself and what she likes to do is always a good opener. Around sixth grade we're actually getting somewhere. We're talking to girls. And they're talking back! When we make jokes now they seem to be laughing in all the right places. We've actually taken our first few baby steps to understanding the fairer sex.

Then summer vacation comes.

And when all the girls come back for seventh grade they have boobs.

And everything we've learned up to that point immediately gets knocked out of our heads.

Yes. Done in by boobs. That's right. It was boobs that done us wrong.

What used to be a simple conversation with a girl can no longer be simple. Or even a conversation. "Hi, Boobra! Uh, Barbara! How was your summer, Boob—*Barb*!" And of course the girl's actual name was probably something more like Pam Hoberman. (I'm so sorry, Pammy!)

Now when a girl starts to talk, a thick London fog blows over our brains.

Can't think. Boobs.

Can't talk. Boobs.

What's her name again? Boobs.

What's *my* name again? Boobs.

I'd like to say we're back to square one, but it's far worse than that. Because boobs completely overtake the part of men's minds where "women knowledge" used to be. Nothing can get in. And nothing can get out. And it's almost like we've never learned anything at all. We revert to maturity levels heretofore unseen in our behavior up to this point. In the cafeteria we giggle as we eat chicken *breast*. In chemistry, we guffaw as we ask a pal to hand us a test *boob*. And thinking we've discovered clever wordplay, we tell everyone it's called alge*bra*! "Get it? Alge-*bra*!"

And thus one more log is thrown onto her crazy fire.

And who can blame her? We've checked out on her just as we were starting to communicate. So when she finally cries out, "You're talking to my boobs!" her mind has already started its slow but steady descent into madness. "But it's not our fault! It's the boobs!" we shout after the girl who's turned her back on us. (Just the first of many women's backs we'll be speaking to over the coming years.) But still, we insist: *Men don't make men dumb. Boobs make men dumb.*

But we know better. One need only look at the evolution of the word "boob." It is now commonly used to refer to a *stupid man*. As in "He's a boob!" Or "What a boob that guy is!" When people say "Can you believe the boobs in Washington?" I can assure you they're not talking about Hillary. To paraphrase the great Al Capp: I have seen the boobs. And they is us.

Now obviously, many boys overcome "boob fog" and go on to have healthy, happy relationships. Unfortunately, many other boys turn into paunchy men who sit on the couch all day watching, yes, the boob tube.

It's also interesting to note that something completely un-expected happens at the juncture where boy meets boob. This is the moment where gay men historically begin to overtake straight men in their knowledge of women. Their keen insight into women and what makes them tick all begins to flower be-cause they're not distracted by boobs. So they can actually *listen* to what women have to say. This is a huge advantage when trying to learn about women. So the people who could actually *benefit* from this knowledge never get it. And the ones who do get it could care less.

The history of stupid and crazy is chock-full of ironies such as this.

DAMN YOU, BOOBS!

In the years immediately following the return of the seventh-grade girls from their summer vacations, the sexes are once again lost to each other for a time. A long time. Yes, there is dating and crushes and making out and things done in cars in awkward positions. But in terms of understanding each other there is very little progress. Junior high and high school serve as a retreat from the great strides we seemed to be making PB (pre-boobs). Girls find solace in newly formed cliques founded often on nothing more than bonding over how stupid boys are. And the boys retreat to their bedrooms and pretty much masturbate until they leave for college.

THE COLLEGE CRUSH

College is where the next great chapter in the history of stupid and crazy is written. Because college is a time of incredible growth for both sexes. It's where stupid boys graduate into stupid men and crazy girls blossom into full-fledged nut jobs. This cementing of our identities is not the tragedy it appears to be at first glance. Because in college we fall in love for real for the first time.

And love changes everything.

Love, or whatever it is that keeps us up late in the dorm room smoking cigarettes, drinking, obsessing, and talking incessantly about our feelings, is as momentous an event as when we first discovered each other's existence on the playground so many years ago. But now the stakes are higher. Because it's love.

And love changes everything.

Men are still stupid, yes. But now we're stupid in the service of love. And there is no higher calling. And if women are driven crazy by love, then so be it. Nothing in the universe is bigger. This isn't about touching boobies or hiding them under big sweaters anymore. We're now crazy and stupid on a whole new level.

THE LESSONS OF ELIZABETH

I was sitting in my required freshman creative writing class. And she walked in. And nothing was ever the same. I was transfixed. To this day, I really don't know why I fell so hard and so fast. It wasn't quite her looks. It wasn't quite her loud, unapologetic personality. It wasn't quite the way she insisted she was "from Philly" when she was actually from southern New Jersey. It might have been her generous laugh, an unselfconscious cackle that seemed to give me the validation I'd apparently been craving my entire life. Whatever it was or wasn't, one thing was for sure: She was the woman of my dreams.

We became fast friends. Then good friends. Then eat-every-meal-in-the-cafeteria-together friends. Then talk-several-times-a-day friends. And then knock-on-each-other's-dorm-room-door-at-any hour-of-the-day-or-night friends.

And then I said I wanted to be more than friends.

And then she said she was fine just being friends.

And then I said I really, really wanted to be more than friends.

And then she said she really, really valued our friendship.

very carefulvery carefully

And then she started talking about Bob. Bob was her high school boyfriend who was now in college in San Francisco. And she seemed to think that she and *Bob* were still "a thing." I seemed to think they weren't.

This was just the first of many misinterpretations on my part. I thought it was obvious that there was something spectacular and life-altering happening between us and it couldn't be denied.

She denied it.

I then set out to *prove* that she loved me as much as I loved her. That's right. I was going to prove to her that what she felt was not love was actually love.

I'd gone to a whole new level of stupid.

Every chance I got I would point out to her how wonderful I was and how happy she was with me. I also never missed a chance to show her how *unhappy* she was with anyone but me—especially anyone named Bob.

She started to get irritated with me.

I started to get irritated that she was so irritated.

She finally told me she was upset that I wanted to have a sexual relationship with her. She considered this a betrayal of our friendship. She was disappointed in me because we were supposed to be friends. I said, "FRIENDS CAN FUCK! FRIENDS *SHOULD* FUCK! IF YOU CAN'T FUCK YOUR FRIENDS, WHO CAN YOU FUCK?!"

Then she said maybe we shouldn't talk for a while.

And we didn't talk for a while.

Then in the middle of the night several weeks later I called her. Sweaty and overwrought, I asked her if anything was ever going to happen between us. That's right. *After being rejected repeatedly for three months straight I asked her to clarify her feelings about our future*. It seems a rather daft question considering all that had gone before. But I persisted nonetheless.

"Is anything ever going to happen between us?"

"No."

"When you say 'no' do you actually mean 'yes'?"

"No."

"No *yes*? Or no *no*?"

Then she sighed deeply and said, "We're parallel lines."

I said, "Whuh . . . ?"

She repeated, "We're parallel lines."

I again said, "Whuh . . . ?"

She said, "Parallel lines. We can get very close but we'll never touch."

That's what she said: *"We can get very close but we'll never touch."*

Even now I feel something akin to getting kicked repeatedly in the groin with a hard-toed shoe when I think of those words. It was the worst thing anyone had ever said to me up until that point. (I've since gone to Hollywood and had much, much worse said to me.) But I was a young man in love. And this burnt a hole through my tender heart.

But thank god she said it.

And said it in that terrible way. Because I finally *got it*. It finally pervaded the all-encompassing fog that was obscuring my brain from all reason. I was finally able to realize that all the time she was telling me she just wanted to be friends, *she actually just wanted to be friends*. It seems a remarkably simple concept these many years later. But love will make you stupid every time. And I was a fool for love. And there are worse things to be. But a fool for love is still a fool.

In the end, what drove Elizabeth nuts was that I simply didn't listen to her. Repeatedly.

Not listening to a woman is the final nail in her crazy coffin.

Men don't listen to women for various reasons. Most often it's because we just don't want to. It's confusing. And loud. And it takes so much concentration. It's like listening to a different language. Who has that kind of time? But when we don't listen to women, they start to feel a lack of trust in us, and guess what it reminds them of? The first day of seventh grade when all we could do was stare at their boobs.

Yes. Stupid on a whole new level just results in the same old crazy.

A *VERY* BRIEF HISTORY OF STUPID AND CRAZY

To review:

We hit them on the playground because we liked them.

Then we made fun of them until they cried.

Then we stared at their boobs.

Then we didn't listen to them. *Repeatedly.*

WHO WOULDN'T BE CRAZY AFTER ALL THIS? So what does this history of stupid and crazy teach us? It teaches us definitively, once and for all, that yes, THE STUPID CAME FIRST. And men all over this universe bear the responsibility of fighting their innate idiocy and making the world a better place for all women. But before all the women reading this march down Fifth Avenue with signs that say THE STUPID CAME FIRST, remember one thing: Stupid can be cured. But crazy is often forever. That's right. Men can get less stupid. It's an arduous process, no doubt, that requires many, many hours of dedicated learning. *But it's still easier than getting less crazy.* And yet, that's what a woman must attempt in order to do her part to bridge the divide with her man.

A woman's sanity can be so fragile that even relatively stable women can get "defensive crazy." The very idea that the man they love is going to act stupid in the future makes them crazy even before he does anything stupid. Yes. They get crazy on spec! This then results in "My man can't ever do right" syndrome, which is a complete disaster.

I told you this was complicated.

But in her first response, I'm sure Jenny will give us all great insight into how a woman's mind actually works.

JENNY'S RESPONSE

A WOMAN'S MIND AT WORK

So this Elizabeth chick, was she pretty?

2

ADMITTING WE'RE STUPID

WHY WE DON'T AND
WHY WE NEED TO

This is my favorite of all the classic genie jokes:

A guy is walking on the beach and finds a bottle. He opens it and a male genie pops out and tells the guy he's granting him one wish. (The guy was hoping for a hot chick genie but a free wish is a free wish, right?) So the guy thinks about it for a minute and then says, "Well, I love Hawaii. But I'm afraid to fly. I want you to build me a highway to Hawaii!" But the genie shakes his head and gets all defensive. "Are you serious? A highway to Hawaii? That's like thousands of miles. And all that asphalt, and all that manpower . . . I mean, that's really, really hard to do. Do you want anything else besides a highway?" The guy thinks about it for a minute and then says, "There is one thing: I don't understand women. Can you help me understand women?" And the genie says, "How many lanes?"

Do you remember the funniest moment in the movie *Tootsie*? (And that's saying a lot considering how brilliantly funny that movie is.) But no matter how much you've forgotten about that classic from 1982, there's one moment that everyone remembers. It's after Jessica Lange has revealed to "Dorothy Michaels"—Dustin Hoffman in a dress—what she really wants from a man. She wants a man to break through all this relationship game-playing and admit he's confused. She says she would love it if someone just said to her, "Look, I could lay a big line on you, but the simple truth is, I find you very attractive and I'd really like to go to bed with you." Then later, Dustin Hoffman, as his regular male character Michael Dorsey, sees Jessica Lange at a party. He goes up to her and says *the exact same thing* she fantasized that her perfect man would say—and she throws her drink in his face.

Nobody gets women.

They don't even get themselves.

God created man and then said to him, "And now for something *really confusing* . . ." Even genies with magical powers are at a complete loss. Women keep us up at night tossing and turning, and in the morning we actually think we have a clue as to what the hell at least one of them is all about, only to be completely befuddled by her before we even get our second pant leg on.

And yet, men can't admit that we're clueless when it comes to women. I, myself, have been reluctant to admit I was a complete dunce about them. I thought success in other areas must presage success in this one. I thought a talent for reason and logic could actually help me. Now I'm sure of only one thing: The stupidest man you'll ever meet is the one who thinks he understands women.

That doesn't mean we stop trying.

But we must recognize the enormity of our task: to get closer to comprehending the incomprehensible. But humility is our friend on this journey. The closer we get to the heart of a woman's mind, the closer we are to realizing we know absolutely nothing. And then we're finally starting to get somewhere.

> A man's gotta know his limitations.
>
> —DIRTY HARRY CALLAHAN, *MAGNUM FORCE*

No less a man than Dirty Harry knows he must admit weakness and human frailty. And yet a man will swear he doesn't need to look at his car's expensive GPS system—even though he insisted on getting it. (Me.) Or that he needs to talk about what's really bothering him—after he's repeatedly pummeled a large chest of drawers. (Me again.) Or that he doesn't need to change his behavior in relationships in the face of mounting evidence that his current behavior isn't working very well. (Guess who?)

But the facts are as they always were: If you're a man, you're stupid about women. Here's the good news: We're not stupid about *everything*. When it comes to knowing facts we can be as smart as the underside of a Snapple bottle cap. But unfortunately, *half of our lives* are spent dealing with women. So for at least half of our time on earth we're raging imbeciles.

A man's gotta know his limitations.

Here's why I spent my stupid twenties and my stupid thirties not admitting I was stupid about women: because I thought it meant I was stupid about *sex*. And nobody wants to be stupid about sex. So I pushed away any thoughts that I might be stupid about women. Not this guy, right? Not Superman-in-the-sack Morris! But in the dark days of my marriage, as the "intimacy" dwindled and then disappeared completely, I feared I might actually be stupid about sex. But then I got divorced. And when I started having sex with other women again, I realized this is not so hard. It's actually pretty easy. You definitely *do not* have to be a college graduate to get this down. I'm not dumb about sex! So I thought I had it all figured out: My ex-wife was just crazy and I'm not stupid about women!

And yet, I still kept pissing off and frustrating women of all kinds.

In my new relationships I kept having many of the same "stupid" issues that I had in my marriage. And then I thought, *Wait a minute, what's the constant here? If you look at this mathematically, 50 percent of any new relationship is still the same. I'm still me, so I must be stupid about something. And if it's not sex, then what is it?* After a few more relationships, I had to face the fact that it was women in general—that would be the other constant.

(Now of course 50 percent of a relationship is the crazy. But we can't do anything about that just yet. Men have to start with themselves. One of the themes of this book that we keep coming back to is: **Take care of the stupid and the crazy takes care of itself.**)

The other reason we hate to admit we're stupid about women is that they're always *calling us stupid.* To their friends, to their mothers, to our faces. And that doesn't feel good. It's humiliating. So, often, we resist the truth in this statement and strike back at them using accusations like "Crazy bitch!"— which always goes over so well—or we just say nothing at all. And neither response really bolsters our case that we're not as they say we are. But frankly, realizing that I was completely obtuse was the best thing that ever happened to me. I found it to be a great relief. At last there's a name for what I have. A diagnosis that makes sense: I'm an idiot!

Unfortunately, it never functions as a very effective excuse for anything.

A man's gotta know his limitations.

Years ago I learned an important reason why we're so loath to admit that we're idiots. An actor, of all people, gave me a great insight into how we need to view ourselves as someone other than who we are. I pitched a pilot for a television show that CBS was so excited about they agreed to produce thirteen episodes before I even wrote the script. The show was about the trials and tribulations of a womanizer who was now getting his comeuppance. (Hollywood executives love characters to get their "comeuppance"—almost as much as they love "a fish out of water." This show had both!) One divorce already behind him, the main character's frat-boy humor was no longer wearing well in his midthirties, and with his mounting business failures, he was forced to take over his recently deceased mother's wedding planning business. It seemed to me that a wedding planning business would be a funny and effective setting for an old hound dog to learn some new tricks. By being surrounded by women—and brides, who are the craziest of the crazies—he'd be forced to get the education he really needed. He would learn how to really *listen* to women while also having to learn about silk shantung.

The script was received by the network with the same enthusiasm as the pitch had been. Now all we had to do was cast it. Who wouldn't love the part of the bad boy womanizer getting his due and learning how to really love women? It was a leading role where an actor could really shine. Lists were assembled by casting directors and the network. We wondered what budding movie star would choose to light up the little screen because he couldn't resist playing this part. Who *wouldn't* want to play this plum role?

Turns out *everyone*.

No actor in Hollywood wanted anything to do with it. Forget movie stars; I couldn't get the guy who shovels shit at the zoo. It was painful to me that no actor with any kind of reputation wanted to play this part that I felt very connected to and was proud to have written.

It wasn't until I had a meeting one day with a popular TV star that it became clear what the problem was. The meeting went extremely well. We talked easily and laughed heartily. Aside from the fact that he was good-looking and charismatic, I was impressed with how articulate and funny this actor was. He said to me at one point, "I know sex with someone you love is better," then paused before adding, "but it's not *that much* better." He was perfect! He *was* the character I'd written! And after spending many years on a highly successful show that appealed to six-year-olds, he was looking for a part that was adult and romantic and would make people forget he'd ever been on that show. He assured me he'd read the script and get back to me.

To his credit he did get back to me. I've had television scripts rejected by every actor in Hollywood. It's routine. (Everyone gets rejected by everyone in Hollywood. It's why we all have such high self-esteem.) But this actor was the only one *ever* to call and talk to me directly about why he rejected my script. In retrospect, I think he really wanted me to understand something. He told me the script was very funny and even quoted some favorite lines, but said what troubled him was that the character "is an idiot when it comes to women." He explained that "actors of a certain age—especially hip ones—don't want to play a guy who's dumb about women." He said that's just not how the leading guy should be. That's the secondary guy. The best friend is the guy who's dense about chicks. He went on to say that no one would buy *him specifically* as a guy who didn't know about women, and he offered as proof the woman he was married to—a well-known gorgeous model/actress.

Point taken.

But maybe if he really knew about women he'd still be married to her.

However, he did make a point about how we view ourselves: We're all the leading man in our own life. Which is a good thing. Who the hell wants to play the sidekick? We're George Clooney. And we can't be dumb about chicks because we got one.

But we've never been stupid about *getting* chicks.

We're stupid about what to do *once we get them.*

That's the hard part. That's where we stop being the leading men in our lives and turn into blithering idiots who should get down on our hands and knees and admit to our god, ourselves, and the women in our lives that we have no clue.

WHY I KEEP QUOTING CLINT

A man's gotta know his limitations—*if he's ever going to exceed them.*

You will never get out of the prison you're in if you can't even see the bars. Like the drunks always say when they get together in a church, the first step is to admit you have a problem. Admitting is the first step to learning, and if you learn something, guess what happens? You're not *that* stupid anymore. Still stupid, yes. But not *that* stupid. And why is being not *that* stupid important?

STUPID/CRAZY EQUATIONS

It all comes down to three mathematical equations:

1) NORMAL WOMAN + STUPID MAN = CRAZY WOMAN

However:

2) NORMAL WOMAN + SMART MAN = NORMAL WOMAN

However:

3) *CRAZY* WOMAN + SMART MAN = CRAZY WOMAN

What This Means: If a man can reduce his stupidity level in his relationship, it will then be matched concurrently with a reduction in his woman's crazy level. A man who reduces his stupidity level, say, 30 percent *should be* able to count on a 30 percent reduction of her crazy. If that doesn't happen, it's safe to assume the woman is just bat-shit crazy and all bets are off.

We have to reduce our stupidity just to figure out what's really going on!

If a man isn't stupid anymore, but she's still crazy, and she wants the relationship to work, guess what she has to do? *Admit she's crazy.* That's right. Admit she's crazy. Most men don't believe they'll ever see the day when their woman admits that she's a major loon. But if a man can truly live by the credo **Take care of the stupid and the crazy takes care of itself,** that day may be closer than he thinks.

JENNY'S RESPONSE

THE ASTERISK*

There he is grinning at me, like a dog who has just laid a bone at my feet. I don't react; instead I just stand there with both hands on my hips looking like the skeptical cousin of I'm-a-little-teapot. He pants a little and then nudges me with his nose as if to say, "Go on, it's your turn, just say it." But suddenly I feel cagey and more than a little stubborn.

"What is it that you want to know exactly?" I'm stalling. I know it. He knows it. But for now he's willing to dance the dance with me.

"Well, I just cast aside my pride and laid myself bare and said that men, me included, are stupid when it comes to women. So now it's your turn to say it."

"Fine. Men, including you, are stupid when it comes to women."

I smile devilishly. After all, it's a perfect setup. I then waggle an imaginary cigar at him and say, "Yuk, yuk, yuk." He is not amused, so I quickly apologize. "I'm sorry. It's just that I don't know what you want from me."

"I want you to admit that women, yourself included, are crazy! C'mon, you know it's a two-way street. It takes two to tango! It . . ." He trails off as he tries to come up with another two-fer saying.

"It takes two for murder-suicide?" I pipe in.

He frowns at me. "Okay, what's your problem?"

This one is not as stupid as he thinks. Yes, he is right. I do have a problem. In the twenty-one years of my dating life I've had lots of men come and go, and even though I'm now in a happily committed relationship, it still has only been a relatively short time that we've been together in the grand scheme of things. Meanwhile, I have some female friendships that have been around forever and really mean the world to me, so I just don't know if I can sell my entire gender down the river with one blanket statement.

"You're being"—he hesitates, carefully choosing his words—"melodramatic. No one is getting sold down any river. I simply want you to admit the truth. I mean, you're the one who said it in the first place. Are you reneging?"

"No, I'm not reneging. It's just that the crazy part is not as simple as the stupid part. *Stupid is, by its very nature, simple!*"

"You're making this way too complicated. All you have to do is admit that you're a little nutty when it comes to men, that's all."

"I don't think I'm making this complicated, I think it *is* complicated. I can't help it that I have a lot of mixed emotions when it comes to this topic, and I just want to sort them out before I go mouthing off, that's all."

"It doesn't have to be emotional if you don't make it emotional," he says matter-of-factly, as if he really believes that you can talk yourself out of your feelings.

All right, now I'm annoyed. I am now speaking through gritted teeth. "I don't *make* things emotional. I don't *make* things complicated. It's not something that I can control. My emotional state does not come with an on/off switch." I watch as he blinks for a second too long, and I know he's thinking, *If only.* If only her emotional state had an on/off switch.

And then suddenly he perks up. "Hey, wait, do you think your inability to control your emotions is what makes you crazy?"

Of all the stupid things to say at a time like this. "Excuse me? I don't have an inability to control my—" And then I stop short. Maybe he's onto something. Maybe that's it. Whenever we chicks hit our crazy point-of-no-return stride, it's usually over something that at its heart is emotional. Maybe women are like Tootsie Pops, where you have to work through a whole lotta crazy just to get to the emotional chewy center. Perhaps the crazy is like a hard outer coating, like armor, something that we employ to protect our emotions with. If we just left our emotions out in the open there'd be a hundred stupid guys stomping all over them. We need that crazy coating!

I take a deep breath. I feel better. I'm ready. "Fine. I am crazy. Women are crazy. Asterisk."

"What?"

"I'll go on the record, but I want an asterisk. You know, so I can qualify it."

"Who are you, Barry Bonds? You can't have an asterisk."

"Sure I can. Here, watch this.*"

"No. That's not fair. I don't have an asterisk."

"This isn't a negotiation! I'm only willing to admit that I'm crazy with an asterisk. Because I'm not just crazy, period. I'm crazy with an asterisk so you can go to the bottom of the page and realize that I'm crazy with emotional justification. Actually, I need two asterisks: one for me, and one for the blanket gender statement."

"No, you're being ridiculous."

"No? You can't deny me asterisks. It's a free word-processing country in case you haven't noticed. Wow, I can't believe you won't give me one. What's it to you? Not like I need your permission to have one, or three.***"

"So now you want three?"

"I want as many as I want. Now I want four!****"

He then gave me the look that said he thought I was crazy, but I didn't care, because I knew I had a reason to be all up in arms. I mean, how dumb to get so worked up over punctuation. Boys are so stupid.[1]

---

[1] The great asterisk debate of 2008 lasted well over an hour and involved me saying the word "asterisk" at least two hundred more times. Howard, not wanting to ever have to hear the word again, finally acquiesced and said to go ahead and use a stupid fu**ing asterisk because he no longer cared.

3

INSIDE THE
STUPID MIND

IS IT THE STUPID ANSWER?
OR THE CRAZY QUESTION?

There is a method to our stupidity.

(Unlike craziness, which is unbelievably random.)

But our stupidity is not haphazard. It follows a pattern. It's deeply ingrained in us. And like everything with men there's a certain logic to it. A certain consistency of thought that we cling to in the face of all evidence to the contrary. We have almost a primitive belief that facts are our friends and that the truth will set us free. So what we say to women makes sense *to us*. And to others like us. It's not stupid to other guys. In fact, when we say something stupid it makes sense in our heads *before* we say it. It even makes sense *while* we're saying it. Only when a grenade is thrown back at us and we realize we somehow have to put the pin back in does its stupidity begin to reveal itself.

So when asked a question by a woman, why is it that we

often seem to say the exact worst thing, at the exact worst moment, causing the woman to ask her friends rhetorically, "Is he just stoo-pid?" (And she knows how the word is pronounced too, she just likes to add the extra "oo" for emphasis.) Then later in the day, still obsessing about her man's feeble response, she exasperatedly asks, "What were you thinking?!"

Here's what we were thinking: *that it was a crazy question.*

Indeed, the major culprit behind stupid answers given by men is insane questions asked by women. Not only are these questions nonsensical, illogical, and downright nutty, but often they require us to read the mind of the questioner in order to give the correct (desired) answer. And mind-readers we're not.

Jenny Lee has an incredible ability to ask me what I call "the Unanswerable Question": the question that begs for an answer but has no good one. And if I foolishly attempt to answer it, it can be extremely hazardous to my health. The double-edged, double-bind question is a staple of the crazy woman. A day before she met my parents for the first time, Jenny asked, "If your parents don't like me, are you going to tell me?"

Just repeating it hurts my head. I pleaded for guidance.

"What do you want me to do?"

"I want the truth."

"The truth it is."

"Unless it's bad."

"A lie it is."

"But you can't lie to me."

"So I just won't tell you anything."

"But if you don't tell me anything then I'll know it's bad."

"So I'll tell you it's good either way."

"But then you're lying to me. I told you, I don't want you to lie!"

"Is there a knife close by?"

"Why?"

"I'd like to stick it in my eye."

What follows is a series of crazy questions that have been asked of me over the years and the conversations that ensued, how they *did* go and how they *should have* gone—in a better world. But don't think for a moment that Jenny asked them all. She's not crazier than the average American woman. But for those keeping score at home, Jenny is responsible for #204, #678, #1, #798, and #4009.

CRAZY QUESTION #204: *Should we tell each other if one of us has an affair?*

"You mean like a *luncheon* or something?" I asked hopefully. No good ever comes from this question. I always come down firmly on the side of not telling.

"But you have to tell me," she says.

"Why?"

"Because I'll find out anyway."

"And what's the advantage of hurrying *that* process?"

"Because if I find out and you *didn't* tell me, then I'll know it *meant something*. And if it meant something, there's no coming back from that."

"But if I tell you—even if it *didn't* mean anything—there's a chance you'll murder me in my sleep."

"You'll have to take that chance."

"How about if I tell you *right after* you find out?"

"Too late."

"Thought so."

And as the seasons turn, the questions keep coming, and our heads keep spinning and threatening to fall off our necks. The painful thing is even when you think you're being smart and answering perfectly, it turns out you're not.

CRAZY QUESTION #678: *If I die, how much time would you mourn me before you moved on?*

"The rest of my life, baby. I couldn't go on. There's no moving on from you."

Sounds pretty good, right? Wrong.

"So I've ruined you forever?" she says. "Being with me is so miserable you're giving up on relationships for good?"

"No! No! I'd just be so devastated—"

"But you *do* have to go on living," she acknowledges.

"You're right. I have to go on living. So I'll live!"

"Okay, okay, enough with the living. I'm barely in the grave and you're dating."

"I'm not dating. I'm just living."

"Seriously, I want you to move on. But factoring in that I'm the love of your life, how long before you do?"

"Hooker at six months. Relationship within a year."

"*Six months after I'm dead you're going to a hooker?!*"

"I'm grieving! It's part of the grieving process!"

"This is how you celebrate my memory? With hookers?"

"If it's any consolation, I really hope I go first. *Now* would be a good time."

CRAZY QUESTION #463: *Do you think my sister is attractive?*

Now, this is extremely complicated territory. I've been asked this question when the sister was a babe and when the sister *looked like* Babe, the talking pig from the movies. And in order to get the exact right answer, one also has to factor in how she *feels* about her sister. (Which also means you actually have to *know* how she feels about her sister.)

Hot-Sister-She's-Jealous-of Answer: "She's okay . . . *I guess*. I mean, she's so not my type. Seriously, you definitely got the looks in the family." But if you happen to give that same answer about her *homely* sister, good luck getting cab fare to the bench in the park where you'll be living.

Homely-Sister-She-Feels-Sorry-For Answer: "Oh, yeah. She's very attractive! Really, really cute! Especially once you get to know her!"

Woe to the man who gets those answers mixed up.

This kind of complexity in answering questions takes a toll on a man's mind. Our brains are just not cut out for all these jumps, reverses, and hairpin turns. It's not that we're simply idiots, it's that a man has to be a freaking *genius* to correctly answer the questions a woman asks him.

CRAZY QUESTION #93: *Which of my friends do you find most attractive?*

Answering this one requires incredible amounts of intellectual gymnastics. A man must first gauge his *actual* level of attraction to her friends; then factor in *her feelings* about her friends' attractiveness; then, after figuring out the one *he's most attracted to,* he must suppress that thought and tell her he's attracted to the one *he's least attracted to*. Only then can he possibly hope for an agreeable response like "You're so right! Marlene has such a pretty face!" If the man stumbles and says he finds her hottest friend attractive, he's charged with being not only an idiot, but a "classic" idiot with no vision. "Everyone goes for Amy with the boobs! You're so typical! Do you have even an ounce of originality?"

When I was a kid there was no hotter woman on the planet than Farrah Fawcett-Majors. If you were twelve or thirteen you were sure to have that famous poster of her kneeling in that red bathing suit, with her very visible nipples, hanging over your bed. Her wild mane of wavy blow-dried hair falling on her shoulders, smiling down on you with her gorgeous extra white teeth as you masturbated. A common refrain of twelve-year-old girls at the time was "Farrah would be nothing without that hair and those teeth." To which boys too often responded, "Who could possibly be good-looking without their hair and their teeth?" In retrospect, I see that this was just the beginning of the crazy statement/stupid response pattern. But as I get older and more mature I realize two things: One, if we'd just shut up and nodded sympathetically, perhaps we could have given comfort to all those girls who were so disturbed by our worshipping at the altar of this "angel." The second thing I've realized is that even with no teeth and no hair Farrah *still would have been hot*.

Now granted, there *are* crazy questions women ask that all men should be used to by now. And they should be able to handle them deftly and graciously. Yes, ladies and gentlemen, I'm talking about *that* question.

CRAZY QUESTION NUMERO UNO: *Am I fat?*

Why It's Crazy: You either are or you aren't. And you know which one it is.

That being said, even the lamest newlywed knows the answer to this perennial question is *always* no. Always. No exceptions. You never tell a woman she's fat. You never *imply* a woman is fat. You never even stand *near someone* who's saying *some other* woman is fat. I'm at Starbucks as I write this and a woman who should know better just asked to try one of their "chocolate old-fashioned" doughnuts. But am I going to say anything? Of course not. And if I was married to her, I would have *suggested* she have the doughnut—even if she wasn't interested in having one. To *not* suggest it is, in a woman's mind, to indirectly tell her she's fat. And yes, for all you following at home, that's crazy!

So this particular question should be a breeze to answer, right? And yet, amazingly, this morning—somewhere in America, far, far away from my house—when a woman asked a random fellow if he'd noticed that she'd put on a few pounds, the guy should have realized that she wanted an honest answer as much as he wants one about whether she's ever been with someone bigger than him.

The Right Answer: "No, baby, you look exactly like you always do. You look great!"

But he didn't say that. For some reason, he actually thought that today was the first day in the history of the world that a woman wanted an honest answer to that question.

The Stupid Answer: "Hon, if you don't feel good about yourself, there *are* things you can do about it."

Yup. That's what he said.

Here's what he was thinking: Maybe she *has* put on one or two. She still looks great, but couldn't we all look better? And heck, if she's really upset about her weight she should *do* something about it. And if I confirm what she already knows, she might just make that Pilates class she's been putting off. And it's not that I don't love her like she is, but wouldn't it be ideal if she felt better about herself? Then she'd be mentally healthier *and* have a tighter ass! It's win-win!

No, no, no.

It's lose-lose.

And he lost-lost.

But what's even more distressing for all of us is that if we can *still* screw up the old "Am I fat?" question—a rookie mistake if ever there was one—where does that leave us when confronted with questions women ask that are far more nuanced in their craziness?

CRAZY QUESTION #798: *Do you really enjoy watching football more than spending time with me?*

The Stupid Answer: What is your fucking problem with football?!

What he was thinking: How can she ask me to compare *her* to a Tom Brady pass on third down? The National Football League is an institution. She's one woman. Granted, she's *my* woman. But it's also *my* league. And this is the ultimate apples-and-oranges scenario. It's like asking me if I like McDonald's more than her. (And of course that comparison can only lead to "You like McDonald's more than me? Fine. Why don't you go sleep with a Big Mac!")

The Right Answer: "Football is just a game, baby. You're the love of my life. Do you want me to rip the cord out of the TV right now? 'Cause I'll rip this thing out right now, I swear. Then I'll smash the screen and take you on a picnic!"

Had he said this he would have immediately quelled her craziness and she would have completely backed off. The man would be back watching football in minutes, and worst-case scenario, she takes a rain check on the picnic.

CRAZY QUESTION #389: *Do you think I'm right? Or do you think your mother is right?*

The Right Answer: "You, baby, you. All you."

The Stupid Answer: "Okay, let's just look at this *rationally.* Mother *does* make a good point—"

Uh-oh. Was that shattering sound a plate over his head?

What he was thinking: *She's my mommy! She makes me special cookies that look like airplanes!*

What he should have been thinking: *I* live *with you. My mother's in Connecticut.*

A QUESTION NONPAREIL

Jenny came home with me to my parents' house in Boston for the first time. She needn't have worried about what they were going to think of her that day they met—they adored her. But still, coming to the place of a man's stupid formative years is stressful for any girlfriend. To add to that stress, my parents invited some relatives over to meet her. At one point I was talking to my cousin's husband when I noticed that Jenny, while chatting with my friend Sherman, was sitting on the love seat alone. And I thought: *Hey! Whoa! My baby is on a love seat with no love!* So I got up, walked across the room, and sat down next to her. As I was sitting I *happened to grab* a handful of nonpareils from a candy bowl on the end table and popped them in my mouth. I then rubbed her lower back. She smiled sweetly at me and said, "That's so nice that you came to sit by me." I smiled back.

CRAZY QUESTION #4009: *Did you come over here for me or for the nonpareils?*

The Right Answer: You, baby, you. You're all the sweetness I need.

And for once in my life I had the right answer! Unfortunately, I also had a mouthful of nonpareils, so it came out more like, "Ooo, aby, ooo. Er all the weetness I eed." She rolled her eyes. I couldn't believe it! I came to her aid and not only did I not get credit, I got *scorned.* (I also kicked myself because if I'd just grabbed the damn nonpareils *after* I'd rubbed her back I'd have had a much more solid defense. But they were those incredible dark chocolate ones from Trader Joe's . . .) Okay, okay, the truth is, I saw the nonpareils and I saw her *at the same time.* So I decided to multitask! Is that so wrong? Aren't women always chiding men for our inability to do two things at once? I was coming to support her *and* getting some candy. *Why can't a man love both?* (I understand how you might *not* be able to love two women at one time. I hear that can get dicey.) But what's wrong with loving a woman *and* a small, flat chocolate drop covered with little white pellets of sugar?! It's not about either/or, it's about love. And that's when I realized: It's about love.

All these crazy questions are about love.

BREAKING THE PATTERN

How can a man stop answering a woman's crazy questions stupidly?

Here's how: A man must understand that the dirty little secret of all those questions about her weight, her sister's attractiveness, his activities once she's dead, his devotion to his mother, and even his love of football and nonpareils can all be boiled down to the one question she's *really* asking: *Do you love me more than everyone else?* That's right. Her big secret agenda is *Do you love me more than everyone else?* And what's so crazy about that? Nothing.

So the next time a woman asks a man if he really enjoys her stories from childhood, and would he like to hear another one, let us just hope—nay, pray—that he suppresses his stupid instincts and keeps the stupid inside for once; smiles at her, knowing what she's really asking him; and says, "Sure, baby, let me put on the tea."

JENNY'S RESPONSE

STUPID SITUATION #6,789

The following is a dramatization of a classic stupid situation between a crazy woman and a stupid man. A lot of men think women are crazy when it comes to their specific needs and wants. I want Polly-O string cheese. The one in the blue package. The one with the little cartoon cow standing on its hind legs that has an expression of mild surprise. What do I get? I get some other string cheese that has a *cartoon mouse* sitting on a block of cheese laughing merrily.

Woman: What's this?

Stupid man: I don't know, what is it?

Woman: It's the string cheese you bought.

Stupid man: Oh.

Woman: I wanted Polly-O string cheese. The one with the cartoon cow. In the blue package.

Stupid man: That package is blue.

Woman: Yes, it's blue. But it's not Polly-O. I can tell by the fact that there is no cartoon cow on the package and that it doesn't say Polly-O.

Stupid man: That one has a cute little mouse on it.

Woman: Yes, I can see that. But I didn't want the one with the cute little mouse. I wanted the one with the cow. I wrote it down on the list. Do you have the list?

Stupid man: I have the list.

Woman: Did you look at the list?

Stupid man: Yeah.

Woman: Can you read me the list?

Stupid man: Look. You wanted string cheese. I bought string cheese. I don't know why you have to get all crazy about it.

Woman: Where is the list? Show me the list.

(The stupid man begrudgingly hands over the list. Woman scans it and begins to read.)

Woman: *"Item number six: Polly-O string cheese!* <u>*Important!*</u> *Must be Polly-O. Blue package. There is a cartoon cow that has an expression of feigned surprise on the package. Do not get me any other kind of string cheese except this one. Not skim. Not lite. Not any other brand. Please."*

Stupid man: Oh. I guess I didn't see that part.

Woman: IT'S IN ITALICS!

Stupid man: I just read the string cheese part.

Woman: But why? Why only that part? Why else would I expound on the packaging and the description if I didn't want it to be read?

Stupid man: I don't know. I guess I messed up. Sorry.

Woman: *How is it possible that you can follow* The Wire *but you can't follow a simple freaking grocery list?!*

This is where the woman then proceeds to go medieval on the guy. Tears, shouting, crying—you name it, she may very well do it. (Or have done it.) Now we all know what he's thinking: String cheese is string cheese, and this woman is totally overreacting!

But is she really?

IT'S THE CHEESE, BUT IT'S NOT THE CHEESE

Upon first glance it's understandable to think of this as a conversation about cheese, and yes, it is about cheese, but it's also not about cheese. The craziness of a woman is like a whole other dimension, but unfortunately there are no glasses that you can put on to see what's really going on. But if there were such glasses, what you would see, if you really studied this situation, is that the emotional center of her craziness is that this man's inability to get her the right cheese is not just standard human error, it's something far, far worse.

Because cheese *is important to her,* she took the time to write very specifically what kind of cheese she wanted. But it's not the fact that she didn't get what she wanted that made her get crazy, it's the fact that *he didn't even try* because he's stupid enough to think that the brand of string cheese doesn't really matter, *because it doesn't matter to him.* But the point that is often overlooked is that the string cheese had nothing to do with him. Because the string cheese was for her. He was just the messenger, a mere vehicle, basically a flesh-and-bone delivery system of string cheese. So the fact that *he* happens to believe that all string cheese is the same is, frankly, irrelevant. No one cares about his opinion on string cheese.

So if you want to know what's happening in her crazy head, it's this: *Just read the list. It's not that difficult. After all, what's a list for but to be read? It really has no other significance at all when you stop and think about it.* I mean, at work does he only *partially* read memos? Just imagine a world where doctors only sort of skim a patient's chart. But maybe on that patient's chart it says that the patient is allergic to penicillin. "Patient will die if given penicillin." So what if the doctor just saw the word "penicillin" and was like, oh, I'll give this patient penicillin. Then what? Well, I'll tell you what would happen. That patient would die. Gone, baby, gone. Flatline Freddy. All because he couldn't be bothered to read all the words on his chart! Who would want such a doctor? Who would feel safe being with a person who has such blatant disregard for another person's health and feelings? Who would want such a boyfriend? I mean, if the guy can't even bother to take two seconds to read a grocery list to get his girlfriend the right kind of string cheese, then there is really no future for this relationship.

Now the woman is wondering whether he even cares about her at all.

Because surely, if he cared about her in the way that she deserved to be cared about, she would, at this very moment, be holding in her hands the right kind of string cheese.

"That wasn't me." Howard states this for the record. "I'm not the Cheese Guy."

"I know it wasn't you. It's just an example."

"An example of a woman going crazy?"

"No, an example of how women see things *emotionally,* especially when a man does something stupid."

"But it was just chee—" I manage to clap my right hand over his mouth just in time. I shake my head. No, dear. Don't even say it. I take my hand off his mouth.

"I was about to say something stupid, right?"

I nod. Yep.

"And then you would have gotten upset."

I nod. Yep.

"Then you would have gone all crazy because you would think that I wasn't paying attention to your emotional outburst."

I nod. Yep.

So now it is time for the million-dollar question. Does he understand that while sometimes cheese is cheese, sometimes cheese is definitely not cheese? He is as nervous as I am. I know he's replaying the story in his head and thinking this is worse than a high school pop quiz.

"I think the takeaway from your story is . . ." I lean in and I find myself crossing my fingers for him. "You were so right, baby, and he was so wrong. His stupid loss was my lucky gain."

Total avoidance on his part, but I don't care. Maybe he knows that right at this moment it's more important to not say the wrong thing, the stupid thing, so instead he suppressed his own feelings on the matter and just said what I wanted to hear, the right thing, the cheesy thing.

4

STUPID CRAZY FREAKIN' ROMANCE

A DRAMA IN THREE ACTS

ACT ONE: THE NIGHT OF THE IGNORAMUS

For two weeks my girlfriend had been telling me that she wanted "a romantic evening out." And I had the perfect opportunity. We were invited to a fancy Malibu party one Saturday night at an incredible beach house just off the Pacific Coast Highway (PCH). It seemed like an ideal setting for romance. The moonlight was sure to be shining down on the glistening water. We'd walk out on the sand, gaze up at the horizon that knows no end. And then when the wind kicked up I'd take off the Armani jacket I'd bought the day before and drape it around her bare shoulders. Then I'd kiss her gently and take her hand in mine like I was never going to let it go.

It didn't exactly go that way.

The party was to celebrate the recent wedding of a great

couple we know, Jonathan Silverman and Jennifer Finnigan.
They're both actors. Beautiful people with beautiful friends.
And we had a really good time at the party. We did walk out
on the beach under the stars, danced a little, ate canapés, and
chatted with Bob Saget. One might even say we had a romantic
time—except for the Bob Saget part. My stupidity began when
I felt the night had been romantic *enough*. Apparently, I grossly
underestimated the *amount* of romance one needs to officially
make it a "romantic evening."

The party started at four, we got there about six, and it
seemed like things were petering out around ten. And we were
both feeling like it was time to leave. She repeated that she
didn't want to go home early. But this didn't seem to register
with me.

MY STUPID DEFENSE LATER: *I wasn't thinking that it was
all that early. It was ten o'clock and we'd already been at the party
for several hours. So since we'd arrived early and stayed for a long
time, I just kind of assumed that meant it was late. At that point it
seemed like we'd had the evening.*

And in fact, she was fine leaving the party but wanted to go
someplace else. She was hungry. At this point my brain should
have sent a signal that said, "Take your baby out and get her whatever she wants!" Unfortunately, the reception was bad in Malibu
that night and the signal I actually received was, "If you can just
feed her quickly, you can get some shut-eye by ten-thirty."

MY STUPID DEFENSE LATER: *You've been saying you've
been tired lately. I figured I should get my baby home. Sue me for
caring about your health.*

So we started to head home but I was actually headed into a perfect storm of male idiocy. Come watch the dark clouds gather from the protection of your own homes . . . We're driving down the Pacific Coast Highway. This is not a depressing road making its way through an industrial wasteland. This very freeway represents romance in our culture. First we pass Moonshadows, a well-known bar and restaurant on the water, and she suggests we pull in for a drink. But I've already passed it and I'm thinking, *Who really wants to make a U-turn* now? I mean, even a romantic guy will tell you U-turns on PCH can be tricky.

MY STUPID DEFENSE LATER: *I was saving your life with the U-turn thing! And you really wanted to go to Moonshadows? Really? That's where Mel Gibson stopped off for a few drinks before his anti-Semitic tirade. How can you be so culturally insensitive?!*

Then we pass Duke's, which is a big sports bar with a full menu of fatty delicious foods and flat-screen televisions on the walls. She's up for Duke's. No Duke's for me. Just not feeling Duke's.

MY STUPID DEFENSE LATER: *I was at Duke's many years ago when Mark McGuire was pursuing Roger Maris's single-season home run record. And I saw him tie the record on one of the big screens at Duke's. And it was a joyous moment then but now seems depressingly naïve given the allegations of steroid use since and his pathetic testimony in front of Congress. Well, hell, how could I possibly go back there?*

We pass Duke's.

Then she notices that all along PCH people have stopped

their cars and are just hanging out looking at the moonlit ocean. They're "parking," she says knowingly. And I understand that "parking" is what I used to call "making out" and the generation before me called "necking."

Still nothing.

MY STUPID DEFENSE LATER: *If you'd just said, "Stop this damn car and do something romantic or I'm going to be unhappy for the rest of our lives!" I would have happily pulled over the car immediately. You just had to say it. Hell, I would have even risked the U-turn at Moonshadows!*

I do manage to remember that she's hungry. And I know a great pizza place nearby. As I pull in I explain that, sure, it doesn't look like much—being sandwiched as it is between a Subway and a KFC—but the pizza is incredible! But the pizza place is closed. We order from a national chain on the way home.

MY STUPID DEFENSE LATER: *They're more reliable. And you get it in thirty minutes. Even if they kill someone on the way over!*

But as we're pulling into the garage, frankly, I'm starting to rethink the whole pizza thing. I mean, she can eat it by herself if she wants but I'm not going to have any. Who needs to be bloated at this time of night? I'm proud that I've made the healthy choice for once.

MY STUPID DEFENSE LATER: *I didn't—I just thought— You're always telling me—Bloated? Bloated, anyone? I'm selling bloated. Anybody buying?*

As we enter the house I'm feeling a bit tired. I mean, I did all that driving on PCH and it is past ten. So I ask her to take the dog out. And when she comes back I'd like her to tell me the consistency of the dog's poopies. Was it firm or soft or pick-up-able? Was it a Tootsie Roll? Or more like soft-serve ice cream?

MY STUPID DEFENSE LATER: *I got nothing.*

In bed that night she keeps saying, "It's fine, it's fine, forget about it," in that sharp, clipped, curt way. But she's tossing and turning so much it feels like I'm on a ship on a dark and stormy night. Finally, she sits up in bed and this is what she says: *"Is it that you don't love me enough? Or is it that your needs always come first? Or is it that you're just too stupid to know what I want?!"*

"THESE ARE MY OPTIONS?" I scream. "THESE ARE MY ONLY OPTIONS?"[1]

JENNY: A year and a half after my marriage ended I met a guy who seemed to have a lot of positive attributes and very few bad ones. So we fell into a heady love affair and after eight short months there was even talk of me moving in with him. He was a writer, like myself, and I found his writing poetic and deeply touching (surely he must have understood romance); he had a big heart, was a big thinker, and seemed to not be bothered by extremes—this is a necessary quality when it comes to dating me and also is necessary for romance. He was playful and fun and entertaining (once we stayed in the presidential suite at Casa del Mar and he had the entire staff call him Mr. President). My number one fear about moving in after such a short time was that he would assume he had

---

[1] Yes, this was the night that launched a thousand miseries and confusions and a relationship crisis so big we needed to write an entire book to figure it out.

"won me" and the romance would stop. Both of us having had marriages end in divorce, we were very verbal about our hesitations and I certainly spoke up about what I wanted.

So imagine my surprise when less than a month after I moved in we had a night that not only lacked in romance but basically took all my hopes of romance *and pounded them into the dirt with a sledgehammer, repeatedly.* Apparently, he doesn't want to be the "dopey guy" who buys flowers for the girl he loves, or be the guy who wears tuxedos, or writes poetry, or pulls his car over so he can stare into my eyes in the moonlight. That's all "cliché bullshit." Instead he'd rather be the guy *who pulls into a Subway parking lot* on the way home when the woman he says he loves says she's hungry and would like something to eat. Never mind that I'm wearing a thousand-dollar dress, spent two hours getting ready, and am wearing high-heeled silver sandals. So while I was hoping that he was looking at me all night and thinking, *How did I ever get so lucky as to land such a beauty for a girlfriend?* he was apparently looking at me like an overdressed dog walker. "Hope she doesn't step in poopies in those shoes, her toes aren't protected." I also want to add one more thing about that night: Our puppy was too young to be left alone for more than a few hours. I had arranged a babysitter for Doozy, with a fixed payment up until one AM and a deal that she'd stay later if necessary at time and a half. I was so excited and certain we'd be out late that I even suggested that she should make a romantic evening of it at our house with *her* boyfriend (going so far as to not-so-subtly imply that I didn't care if they did it on our couch, because everyone should share in the bliss, as I knew I'd be parking in a Prius along PCH with my honey). So when I was paying her at 10:37 PM I knew she felt bad for me, and I felt bad that she felt bad, not to mention totally mortified. The only thing worse than being all dressed up with no place to go is being all dressed up and brought home so early that the sitter feels sorry for you.

ACT TWO: THE FALLOUT

HOWARD: So I sit up next to her in bed and say something to the effect that romance isn't really my thing and that she shouldn't take it personally.

JENNY: I then explain to him that *his self-image* isn't what's at stake here, and in fact it seems he's missing the whole point of everything in the entire world (I am and will always be prone to slight exaggerations). "Romance is not about you," I say.

"Great," he says, "so then I guess we're done talking."

HOWARD: Sometimes levity can really relieve a stressful situation. Sometimes not. (And it does have to actually *be* levity.)

JENNY: I always respect a guy who'll give me a little lip back. (Of course it's a very fine line between getting respect from me and getting dumped by me.) But I wasn't finished with him—until I was finished with him, if you know what I mean.

"You not wanting to be some dopey guy who shows up with flowers is a very selfish idea because you're only worried about *yourself*. Romance is putting another's needs in front of your own, and it would be best if it was at a cost." By "cost," I explained, I wasn't talking money. I meant the romance quotient is upped by the amount of effort that is exerted in blood, sweat, and tears.

"Actual blood, sweat, and tears?"

"WHAT?! AM I NOT WORTH A LITTLE BLOOD, SWEAT, AND TEARS? YOU THINK LOVE SHOULD BE EASY? THAT ROMANCE IS ALL ROSE PETALS AND COTTON CANDY? WELL IT'S NOT. HOW CAN YOU NOT UNDERSTAND? ARE YOU REALLY THIS STUPID OR ARE YOU JUST STUPIDLY PRETENDING TO BE STUPID?"

In retrospect, I should have just pounded it into his head by borrowing his romance-killing sledgehammer.

HOWARD: In retrospect I wish she had.

Instead we stayed up all night fighting, screaming, crying, arguing, and talking about our feelings. Much of the long night remains a blur. But certain things come back to me like a jarring sudden flash in a dark room: Jenny insisting that she could *prove* to me that I loved frozen yogurt more than her; me playing nervously with her hair clip, which at a particularly tense moment suddenly popped out of my hand and hit her right in the eye. (Even at the height of our misery she still managed to crack us up by screaming, *"See? It's all fun and games until someone loses an eye!"*) But mostly what I remember is her wailing, "Why? Why? Why?" in a terrible heartbreaking refrain: "Why? Why? Why?" she wanted to know. "Why? Why? Why?" she asked me as if she were a child and I'd just told her that her supercuddly favorite rabbit's foot was actually a *rabbit's foot.*

"WHY? WHY? WHY?"

HERE'S WHY: "The wedding party freaked me out!"

I told her. Weddings are a hotbed of women acting crazy and men acting stupid. Even she couldn't dispute that weddings bring up issues. And really romantic weddings are the worst. It suddenly puts an unfair spotlight on a couple's own romantic situation. How does your relationship measure up to that of this beautiful couple against this idyllic backdrop? Are you the couple who "used to be like" the beaming bride and groom? And if you're not married, are you developing a cold playing Adelaide to his Nathan Detroit? And this wedding party *in particular* had pumped up her crazy and jacked up my stupid—my stupid being more jacked than her crazy was pumped.

Jonathan Silverman and Jennifer Finnigan are the most romantic couple in the world. Not only were there hundreds of people celebrating their marriage at this little beach party, but they'd already had not *one,* but *two* romantic weddings. This was essentially their third wedding! They got married at a vineyard in Napa Valley and then again under the stars on a gorgeous Greek island. Enough already! We get it! You're married!

She stared at me but now with dead eyes.

"Are you actually *blaming Jonathan Silverman for your behavior tonight*?"

"I'm just saying he has to take his fair share."

"Blame him for the movie version of *Brighton Beach Memoirs*!" she said, her voice rising. "BUT DO NOT BLAME JONATHAN SILVERMAN FOR YOU BEING AN ASSHOLE!"

So much for the vaunted Silverman Defense.

She stared at me in horror for an uncomfortable amount of time. Then she went for the jugular. *"You're even worse than Maalox Guy!"*

She meant it as a blow and it was.

"Maalox Guy" was the name she'd given to the boyfriend of a good friend of hers. Her friend was particularly sweet and wonderful to this guy when he suffered a stomach ailment that killed another in a series of romantic nights gone awry. So to make up for that night and thank her for being so sweet and understanding, what did he do? Well, he didn't give her flowers. Or even chocolates. Instead he gave her a bottle of Maalox with a bow on it. He thought that was romantic. *In a cool way.*

He's now her ex-boyfriend.

Personally, I felt for the guy. But he violated the most basic rule of romance. He made it about *him*. He put a bow on the thing *he needed* that night he'd been sick. She was kind of hoping that he might put a bow on what *she* needed that night—some flowers. He also tried to outsmart romance, to somehow reinvent it. But you can't outsmart something you don't really understand. I know women all across America are still wondering, *Dude, how do you go with the Maalox bottle over flowers?* In his defense, he'd finished her bottle of Maalox that night and thought he was replacing it in a cute way. And I don't know him, but I'm guessing if you asked him about it, he'd say that flowers are Hallmark bullshit. The Maalox bottle was clever in an edgy and unique kind of way. And it was funny!

I know what he'd say because *I would have said it too.*

Which is why I was now being called Maalox Guy by my girlfriend—and it wasn't a compliment.

And so it went. All night long. Accusations, tears, anger, and dreary silences. In the end we did get through it. I mean morning came. The sun did rise. At least there was *that*. But when we finally awoke I was determined to make up for my romantic abomination. And I wasn't headed to the drugstore.

JENNY: Howard did the full-court press of apologies that next week: flowers, a giant balloon bouquet, and a cookie basket.

HOWARD: Jenny stopped me before I threw my life savings into a life-size Lego statue of her that you can get for just sixty thousand dollars from the Neiman Marcus catalog. She appreciated my peace offerings and we reached a dé-tente of sorts. But the issues revealed that night remained. And with every passing day there was a building unrest in our house. It was clear that I didn't understand something very basic about her and important to her core being. This was a big one for her—probably *the* big one—and I wasn't getting it.

JENNY: There *was* this lingering feeling that something was very, very wrong in Howard and Jenny Land. If we'd seem-ingly put it to bed for the night, this was no sleeping dog, this was the Loch Ness Monster of relationship problems, and soon enough we were once again discussing what neither one of us wanted to discuss.

HOWARD: Romance. Yes, romance. Oy, romance.

Romance is the big one: the Alamo of all the things that divide men and women. Here's the truth about men and ro-mance: *We just don't get it.* We don't relate to it. And we certainly don't yearn for it in the same way. We don't want to be swept off our feet by some Princess Charming and ride bareback on a white horse on the beach.

JENNY: I must admit this topic makes me cranky. It's come up in every relationship I have ever had and I hate talking about it. Romance is one of those things that is sacred, like something only to be whispered about while lying on a large velvet Moroccan daybed surrounded by pillows or written about in letters that are tied up in ribbons and sitting in a shoe box in the back of a closet. Romance is not something that should have to be explained the way you would explain that when you wash laundry whites go with whites and colors go with colors. And it's not even something to be discussed logically or analytically, or diagrammed in chalk on a blackboard with X's and O's as if you're discussing strategies for winning a football game.

HOWARD: This is what I just heard: blah, blah, blah, *football*.

JENNY: Howard is suddenly alert and smiling; he is sitting taller and I'm sure his heart is pumping a little bit faster at the mention of his favorite American pastime. It's incredible. One moment we're having a frustrating conversation about romance (and how I want more of it) and he's bored as hell, and the next moment I see his eyelids fluttering and I can tell his breathing is heavier and all because of the mere mention of freakin' football. What about me? Why can't you get excited about going out with me the way you do when you think about football? Instead of the countdown to kickoff (the first Thursday after Labor Day weekend), what about the countdown to when you get to see me again? What about making a pass and tackling me?

HOWARD: I can do that last thing. But if romance was really just about making a pass and tackling, a lot of guys would be better at it. But it's not about making a pass and tackling, it's about all the stuff that *leads up to* the pass and tackle.

It's the Richard Gere part we don't get.

By the way, I blame him for this whole romance mess we're in—along with Jonathan Silverman. Richard Gere is the one storming into factories in uniform to carry away his lady to a better life and lift her up where she belongs. He's the one popping his head out of limos and climbing fire escapes to get to his pretty woman. In his latest movie he and Diane Lane are kissing on the beach with horses galloping in the background! (Doesn't he even remember that other movie where Diane Lane cheated on him with the sexy Frenchman Olivier Martinez?! I guess the Dalai Lama has taught him about forgiveness.)[2]

JENNY: I get it, I swear I do. Romance has nothing to do with reality, so how is it that we girls expect our boys to deliver it in the real world? I suppose this is where the crazy part comes in, but let me be clear: I don't think it's crazy for a woman to want romance (it's genetic and we just can't help it). I will

___

[2] Jenny and I were looking at the movie page in the paper the other night and saw that an ad for *Nights in Rodanthe* was opposite an ad for the Ed Harris Western *Appaloosa*. The tagline for *Nights in Rodanthe* was "It's never too late for a second chance." The tagline for *Appaloosa* was "Feelings can get you killed." Who do you think wanted to see which movie? We ended up staying home.

concede that perhaps we chicks can be a smidge irrational when it comes to our expectations for romance. But when it comes to this topic I will always be irrational and I will always be stubborn. I want to believe in it. I want to care about it. I want to dream that there is a white knight out there who finds my petty and frivolous demands utterly charming, a guy who really knows me, knows what I'm thinking, and will actually answer "you" instead of "nothing" when I ask what he's thinking about.

HOWARD: That's such an easy one and I always screw it up! When they say, "What are you thinking about?" just say, "You!" It's not like whatever we're really thinking about is important anyway.

JENNY: We can't possibly already be that couple who are so starved for romance that we're sitting across from each other in a crowded restaurant not talking, and not in that comfortable silence way, but in that horrible oh-my-god-we-have-nothing-more-to-say-to-each-other-and-I-can't-believe-I-have-to-find-another-boyfriend-no-I-just-can't-do-it-again-oh-I-know-maybe-we-should-take-ballroom-dancing-classes-together way. That's it. I'm tired of these games that couples play. I'm sick of being a broken record. I don't think I'm wrong in wanting what I want, but maybe the failure is partially mine because I can't convey what I'm looking for in a way that he understands.

HOWARD: And that's what she set out to do. Explain romance in a way that I would really understand. Good luck to her!

ACT THREE: THE ROMANTIC EDUCATION OF HOWARD J. MORRIS

JENNY: First I decided to offer Howard a real-world example of romance: This is a tale of a man behaving *beautifully* as opposed to *badly*. It's also positive reinforcement! And this is not an urban legend that happened to a "friend of a friend"; it happened to an actual friend of mine (my best friend, Laura). And I didn't just hear about it; I was there and witnessed it myself.

HOWARD: I'd heard this story six hundred times before but there was a slight difference this time: *I was listening.*

JENNY: It was Laura's wedding day and the newly married couple were blissfully happy after making their commitment to each other in front of two hundred of their closest friends and family. Their first dance as husband and wife was to Dean Martin's song "You're Nobody Till Somebody Loves You" from the *Swingers* movie soundtrack. This was a song they danced to on one of their first dates; it's the song they used at their ballroom dancing lessons; and it's the song she heard every day in her head leading up to her wedding when she thought about her first dance. No one knew this at the time, but when they danced their first dance it was not the right version of the song (due to a snafu with a DJ who swore he had the right version). They danced beautifully and it seemed perfect. But yet, it wasn't exactly perfect for Laura, as she was a little upset that it wasn't the right song. And yes, sure, she knew that such a tiny little detail didn't really matter in the grand scheme of the occasion, but it just wasn't exactly how she had imagined it to be.

Chris, now her husband, knowing her and understanding her disappointment, secretly dispatched two of his loyal groomsmen to a local mall, where they procured the right version of the song from a Best Buy. He then made a speech telling us all what had happened and how he managed to mend the situation, and that he felt lucky that he was the guy who was able to make all her dreams come true not only on this night, but hopefully every night for the rest of their lives.

Deafening silence. Crickets. Pins dropping. All the women were holding their breath listening to him and blinking back tears over the thoughtfulness of his gesture. The men were silenced too, but in a different way. Their breath was taken away because they were pissed that Chris had just set the bar a little out of everyone else's reach. Just like that.

HOWARD: That Chris.

JENNY: My now ex-husband (we were married at the time of this wedding) never forgot that moment either, and interestingly enough he's the one who usually brought it up in conversations in the years afterward. He would say it was a shining example of how one man ruined the life of every other man in the room. I never quite understood his line of thinking. It just didn't make sense to me that I could see the story as something wildly romantic when he saw it as something totally negative. I mean, why not use it as an example to aspire to in the future? Why wouldn't you want to be the guy who not only wins the heart of the girl of his dreams, but also wins the affection of every woman in the room?

HOWARD: I want to be that guy! Why can't I be that guy? I can be like Chris!

JENNY: Apparently, there are *some guys* who find romance to be too much pressure. I suppose this is how my ex-husband felt, but he's *no longer around* so I guess I don't know for sure. After my marriage ended I had no idea what I wanted for my next relationship, but I sure as hell knew what I didn't want. I did not want a guy who was stupid when it came to romance.

HOWARD: Then I got defensive. Because at that point she'd blown past the "inspirational/aspirational" part of the story, dropped her whole positive reinforcement tactic, and was back to the whole bitter-about-that-night thing.

Look, I know I was a total dick that night.

And there's no one to blame for my shoddy thoughtless behavior but myself. And I really do want to learn how to be the romantic guy she wants me to be. *But I can't learn in a hostile environment.* So I went on the attack! (Unfortunately, if one is attacking it helps to have some real ammunition—not just one of those toy guns where the funny sign drops down when you pull the trigger.) "You like to parade around as Little Miss Romantic Pants, don't you?" I started off strongly. "But when I first put myself out there and said I loved you, *you scoffed at me!*"

"I scoffed at you because you *didn't say* 'I love you'!"

"I did too!"

"You said, 'I *purple* you'!"

"YOU KNEW WHAT I MEANT!"

JENNY: It was the first overnight trip that I ever went on with Howard and his son, Dustin. Dustin was six at the time and we drove two hours away to go to this tram that will take you up a mountain where you can actually see snow. This is an exciting proposition for any Californian because we barely get any rain, let alone snow. So we are atop the mountain and in the gift shop and both Dustin and I bought the Star Moodstone necklace.

I've always liked mood rings. Sure, I understand that there is a scientific explanation about how and why they change colors, but to me they still seem a little magical. Being neurotic and crazy, I am always thinking and feeling any number of things and emotions at any given time, so I welcome the color-coded cheat sheet on how I'm feeling. If it's black I'm unhappy and stressed. If it's green I'm normal and relaxed. (I'm rarely ever considered normal, so green really makes me happy.) Blue means I'm excited and happy, and according to the Star Moodstone necklace, purple means love.

And while Dustin and I were excited by how often the colors changed, it seemed pretty consistent that we were both in predominantly purple moods. Dustin, being six years old at the time and a happy kid, was very excited by this. To him, I'm assuming, purple means that he is loved, which is a good thing (as love probably means ice cream in the future, which I feel is six-year-old logic), but for Howard and me (then forty-two years old and thirty-five, respectively), in a new relationship, love was a bit more complicated.

I'm not sure who said it first, but I'm willing to put money down that it was Dustin who said, "I purple you." It sounds like a six-year-old, right? And when a six-year-old says he purples you and has the Star Moodstone necklace to prove it, what choice do you have but to check your own Star Moodstone (it was purple) and say it back? "I purple you too!"

Howard did not buy a Star Moodstone necklace; it's sort of not his thing. I'm not saying he had outgrown the concept, but he's a man whose moods change so rapidly he probably feared the stone might explode from the overload. But because he was relieved that our trip was going well, he was getting regular sex, he was happy, and *we* were happy, he jumped on the "I purple you" bandwagon.

So pretty soon we were all saying it and all meaning it, but in Howard's case he had no real proof, and I guess he was expecting me to just go on faith that it was true. But how could I when I had proof of my own feelings, and Dustin's feelings, but I was just supposed to wing it with Howard?

Howard continued saying "I purple you" for several days after we got back from the trip. At first it was cute because it signified that he had had as much fun as I had. But after a while I realized that this was his way of saying that he loved me without *really* saying it—which is when I stopped finding it as cute anymore.

To me he was saying, "I love you, but only as long as your moodstone says you love me and my imaginary moodstone says I love you, but that's as far as I'm willing to go at this moment in time." I mean, who is to say that he couldn't look down one day at his imaginary moodstone and think, *Uh-oh, it's orange, which means I don't love you and that I need more vitamin C?*

The best part about being six is that you are in the moment because you don't actually understand time and the concept of a future, nor even do you understand commitment. Telling someone you love them is simple and pure and comes with no strings or baggage. But as a forty-two-year-old divorced man with commitment issues, saying "I love you" meant a great deal more. Was the whole "I purple you" thing his training wheels? His safe way to tell me that he loved me but just in case I didn't purple him back he was still going to be okay? What would be next, a bubblegum-machine ring and an "I wuv woo" said in the voice of Scooby-Doo?! There is a time for baby talk and a time to say it like a man. (The time for baby talk in my book is when you are talking to an actual baby.) When he protested against my protest, he said he thought I would think it was cute. I said I did think it was cute—*from a six-year-old.*

HOWARD: Fine. The purple thing was lame. But I might have had her if I'd done my best Scooby-Doo voice. "I *rooby rooo* you!" Needless to say, the famous Chris story didn't have its intended effect and once again we were both left feeling unappreciated and misunderstood. I had some moments over the next few months when I seemed to be getting it—flashes of almost Gere-like brilliance—only to once again fall off into the not-getting-it abyss. I now knew romance was about the grand gesture as well as the small subtle one. It was about effort, selflessness, the art of surprise, pretty things, and doing it all with a touch of theatricality. None of which I've ever been good at. *But I knew that was also the point.* (That would be the effort and selflessness part.) In our many discussions I was also shocked, frankly, to learn that love and romance are *not the same thing.* I'd always assumed they were. And if you had one then who needed the one with the flowers? I also learned that romance isn't sex—although done well it certainly leads to sex. (Which makes one wonder why more men aren't better at this.) The knowledge wasn't easy in coming; you'll notice the issue poking its pretty little head in several of the remaining chapters. But I knew it was a subject too important to give up on. And luckily Jenny wasn't about to give up on me. As far as us trying to figure it out together, it was game on. Literally.

LOVE IN THE TIME OF HD

JENNY: I was staring at the TV—at a football game of all things—when it hit me. "That's what I want." It was suddenly clear to me.

"What?" he asked, unable to mask his "Why are you talking to me during football?" voice. And in truth we'd made a deal that when he's watching a football game I actually have to let him watch the football game. And all conversations have to be game or snack related. But this was too important.

"It has to do with football," I said tantalizingly.

"I'm listening."

Well obviously, football has nothing to do with romance when it comes to what I think of when I think of romance, but I do think that when it comes to men and their sports and their HD TVs, it might be a very similar notion.

Just follow the bread crumbs for a moment:

We have a really large flat-screen TV—really large. I was there when it was picked out and we weren't on the main showroom floor staring at the rows and rows of little TVs; no, when Howard bought his TV we were ushered into the back room that is reserved for "special clients," where we got to sink into a plush leather couch and stare at the dream TV. The one that costs beaucoup bucks; the one that the reviewers crowned the best; the one that is so fancy that it has the name "Elite" in the title.

HOWARD: My father refused to get our family a color TV well past the time when it was already a staple in the American home. *Decades past.* He kept telling my brother and me that they hadn't really "gotten color TV down yet," that the colors weren't right and they only had like three colors anyway. Not like our trusty black and white twenty-nine-inch Sylvania, which, he maintained, had a superior picture to any color TV. *Did he not think we had friends?* It was the same absurd rationale that also denied our family a VCR, even though he wanted one so he could tape all his beloved Charlie Chan movies. Finally, my mother had to threaten to leave him if he didn't buy one already. So the big TV with the perfect picture has always been part of my American dream.

JENNY: I'm not really making fun, even though it sounds like it; Howard works really hard for his money and he deserves to spend it however he wants. And I'm not the girlfriend who is putting her hands on her hips and thinking, *There goes my new washer and dryer;* no, I'm the girlfriend who's like, "Get it. You deserve it." (Because god knows, I don't deny myself when it comes to designer handbags.) So he gets it, and we get the built-in cabinets to store the DVDs. We get the Blu-ray player; we get the booster upgrader magnifier deluxe ultra-maximizing-super-duper thingamajiggy that makes channels that aren't HD look a little better;[3] we get a new stereo; we get the deluxe surround-sound speakers (which come with five new holes in our ceiling); and we get the remote control that needs to be programmed by a pale kid who just graduated from a technical college. This wasn't just a new TV, this was a new way of living. Howard was beyond excited, like a kid in a candy store, like a puppy with a bag full of bones, like a man who just bought a large-screen plasma TV that is fit for a king.

And there we are watching it when I notice something interesting. It's a night game and the New England Patriots (Howard's hometown and favorite team) were playing some team that I can't remember (though I do remember that they had very attractive cerulean-blue uniforms—the Chargers? the Titans?). It's a home game for the Patriots and it's a crisp fall night and the sky is very inky black and you can see the steam coming out of the mouths of the capacity crowd at Gillette Stadium, which is causing an iridescent halo to surround the whole stadium, almost like they are playing in a galaxy far, far away. Howard is pointing out how clear the picture is, how sharp the lines are—this is his new MO ever since we got the TV: "Have you ever seen such a picture?"

I am ignoring him but I am finding myself mesmerized by

---

[3] HOWARD: It actually upgrades regular *DVDs* to look more like HD, not "channels." But just the fact that she's talking all technical is making me fall in love all over again.

the screen. I'm leaning forward and squinting. "This looks better than real life," I say. He immediately responds that this isn't real life, it's HD. I let him know that *I know* it's HD, but what I'm saying is that the picture *looks better than real life.* Meaning, I'm pretty sure that if we were at the game right now what we would see with our own two eyes wouldn't look this vivid. He agrees. It's actually probably better because it's lit a certain way and the cameras filter light differently, pixels, color, blah, blah, blah, techno jargon that I don't understand or care to learn about.

"And you like it this way?" I ask him.

"Of course. This is what I always wanted since I was a small kid. Have you ever seen such a picture?"

"That's it. *That's exactly what romance is,*" I say. "It's those moments in life that are in HD."

I clearly have his attention. Whether I have his *comprehension* is another matter. But attention is good. I'm happy with attention! I find myself suddenly hopeful. I used to believe that a man who doesn't "get" romance will probably never get it, but maybe it's a knowledge gap that can be overcome after all. If he can see this picture, then maybe it's possible he can see the pictures that are in my head and heart, the ones that I see when I think about romance.

As I start to explain my latest theory, he stares at me like I'm a wind-up toy on the floor that has a little more staying power than expected. I know he doesn't understand me at times. I know at times I'm not being rational and most people wouldn't understand me. But what he has learned is that I don't have a tendency to rant for no reason, and that it's in his best interest to try to pay attention as best as he can because it's obvious something is going on and it's highly unlikely I'm going to let it go. So he just listens, for this is now his fate as my boyfriend. He sits and listens, hoping he can soon find that shiny needle in my complicated crazy haystack. (Which he may just use to poke his eyes out.)

"Don't you want our love life to be in HD?"

"I don't understand the question. But I want everything to be in HD, so yes."

"What I'm looking for is *our* life, *our* relationship, but in high definition. So it's clearer, sharper, looks better, sounds better, and I'm lit to look like I'm really skinny and have great cheekbones."

He's thinking about this.

"I'm just saying that sometimes I want us—but a better version. What I had wanted on that fateful night was for us to still be us—a couple really in love, but the HD splashy special version of us instead of Howard and Jenny at home on a Saturday night. I wanted 'Howard and Jenny All Dressed Up in Malibu'; 'Howard and Jenny Live from the Beach on the Night of a Full Moon'; 'Howard and Jenny Use the Magic Romance Time Machine and Go Back to Each Other's Proms.' Hell, I would have done 'The Howard and Jenny Remake of the Falling-in-Love-in-the-Snow Montage from the movie *Love Story*.'" Uh-oh, I'm losing him, I think fast. "OR 'Howard and Jenny on a Runaway City Bus with a Bomb On It!' in HD."

It's almost as if I can see into his brain—which I imagine to look like the children's board game Chutes and Ladders; I see the spinner coming to a stop, his game piece being moved the appropriate number of spaces and up, up, up he goes on a ladder, and it seems that he may have an inkling of understanding.

"So you're unhappy with our relationship?"

But then he lands on a chute and down, down, down he goes and we're back to square one. This is why romance makes me cranky.

HOWARD: No, no, I think I'm getting it! Okay, I'm getting *something.* (Whether it's "it" I have no idea.) After all, this is a conceptual idea and I usually like my ideas with more meat and potatoes. But I certainly understand the beauty of HD. And she's right it isn't like real life—it's better. And I also get that everyone deserves to see the world in HD, if only for a moment. Certainly Jenny and I have had some HD moments in our two years together, when everything around us seemed to have a wonderful heightened sense of reality to it. Our first New Year's Eve comes to mind. We were at a restaurant downtown on a high floor with a great view of downtown Los Angeles. But the view was only the shimmering background to the shooting star that was Jenny Lee that night. And everything from the neon signs out the window to the restaurant's silverware did look clearer, brighter, and just simply *better.* It was one of those nights when you can't believe how lucky you are to be with this particular person in this exact moment in time.

And I know that Jenny wants me to see her in well-lit HD. *But that's how I see her.*

But I have to get her to *see* that I see her that way. (And more than just on New Year's Eve.) So I guess I just have to show her. Every day. Or certainly more days than I've been doing. And now we're back to the practical: the effort part. The planning. The creativity. The knowing what she wants and going the extra mile to give it to her. I guess it's still hard for me to reconcile the odd recipe for romance, whose top two ingredients seem to be the magical *and* the practical. The spontaneous and the completely planned. The real and the ethereal. You have to whip up the fantasy and the reality just right to make this soufflé rise.

And now that I'm making dessert metaphors we're in conceptual territory and I'm totally lost again! Give me some meat and potatoes, woman!

YOKO LOVE

JENNY: I knew what I had to do: I had to tell it to him like a man. I had to cross over to his side and just say it directly, plainly, and in a way he'd understand. (And if that didn't work then maybe I would just have to pop him in the snoot. Joking.)

"I want Yoko Love."

"What?"

"The way John Lennon loved Yoko Ono. I want that."

"You want to be loved in a way that broke up the Beatles?"

"Yes."

"The Beatles, as in the best band in the history of the world, but you wouldn't care if they broke up over you?"

"I would not care."

"You're saying you would break up the Beatles?"

"I'm saying that there is no doubt that he loved her."

"But she broke up the band!"

"She did."

"And you find that romantic."

"In a way that I wish I didn't. But yes, secretly, I do. He loved her. He chose her. There is always a cost."

"By cost you mean *breaking up the Beatles*? That's a helluva cost."

HOWARD: Incredibly, just the day before I'd seen a bumper sticker that said STILL PISSED AT YOKO. I laughed when I saw it because I felt the same way. Now I was being asked to go to the other side. To be the one who breaks up the Beatles! In an alternate universe, the one that Jenny would have us live in, that bumper sticker reads STILL PISSED AT HOWARD.

JENNY: He's aghast. I'm sort of feeling a bit queasy myself. I can't believe I'm saying this out loud. I can't believe it's come to this: romantic hardball. He says, "So you're saying you'd be happy if I started a band, became world-famous with our music inspiring millions of people, and then I gave it all up for you while losing some of my best friends from childhood?"

"I'm saying I'd find it romantic."

"You are one crazy broad."

"I know."

HOWARD: Of course the bumper sticker I'd seen had it wrong. It was John who broke up the Beatles. Not Yoko. His love for Yoko clearly dwarfed his love for Paul—whom he'd had enough of by this time anyway. But doesn't Jenny understand what breaking up the Beatles wrought? Aside from John going into semi-retirement, only to come out occasionally to tell us he was "watching the wheels go round and round," it brought something far more devastating into our lives: Wings. Paul McCartney's post-Beatles band with his wife Linda. It was like Paul was saying, "You're going to break us up over a chick? I'll start a band with *my* chick!"

Is that what Jenny wants? For us to be Wings? A completely inferior band to the Beatles? Is that love? Is *that* romance?! The Beatles produced *Abbey Road* and the White Album. Wings gave us "Silly Love Songs"!

Wait a minute.

Is that what this is all about?

Silly love songs?!

Jenny and I have vastly different tastes in music. She rarely ventures outside the sugary Top 40. I like a little more substance and a harder edge to my music. But this isn't about me, is it? (Later I logged on to iTunes and of course "Silly Love Songs" is the bestselling Wings song of all time.) So I downloaded it. And guess what? It's as bad as you remember.

It has a weird seventies, toe-tapping, head-bopping beat. Later, in a strange interlude in the middle of the song, Paul and Linda sing a round. (Like "Row, Row, Row Your Boat.") But he keeps singing, *"How can I tell you about my loved one?"* while she sings, *"I love you."* Then he takes over *"I love you"* duty and she tells us about *her* loved one. But before the two lovers can conclude their unabashed love fest, there's a rocking disco section that only Deney Terrio could love.

It's terrible, yes.

But a kind of beautiful terrible, too. And there's something oddly *authentic* about it—as there always seemed to be about Paul and Linda's relationship. Jenny may be a John-and-Yoko girl, but I've always had this admiration for Paul and Linda that even I don't understand. It seemed to me that in pictures of them there was always this intimacy that couldn't be faked. And her death in the prime of their lives was so tragic, I never thought Paul would get over it. (And judging from who he married and divorced, I don't think he has.) But I always saw Paul and Linda's relationship as kind of, well, dare I say it . . . *romantic.*

And suddenly "Silly Love Songs" didn't seem so silly.

Or as Paul might say *"It isn't silly. It isn't silly. It isn't silly at all!"*

It's a Jenny Lee song if ever I've heard one. I can see her singing it while dancing around the house. And believing its message of love songs for their own syrupy sweet-tasting sake. *Some people want to fill the world with silly love songs. What's wrong with that?*

Indeed.

JENNY: Who knows if he really got my Beatles analogy. Who knows if he ever will. But what I realized in that moment is that I take love and romance very seriously. It's how I want to live my life. I did not choose to become a corporate lawyer like my parents wanted me to be. I chose to struggle and try to become a writer. I did not settle for a mediocre marriage. I chose to leave my husband with hopes for something better. It's not that I expect it to come all my way and go only in one direction. I am more than willing to be the one to lay down my coat across the mud puddle in the street so Howard doesn't get his brand-new New Balance sneakers dirty. I am willing to put myself out there even if I don't come out smelling like roses. Really out there. I don't want to be the one who's sitting on the couch on Saturday night watching a great picture; I want to live it. I want to be walking on the beach with our pants rolled up, holding hands when four wild horses storm past us (the typical symbolic representation of heightened romance and sexuality). I want him to say, "Have you ever seen such a picture?" and he's talking about the way the moonlight has lit up my face (so I look like I have fabulous cheekbones) and he's talking about me. Us.

He is not saying anything and I try my best not to ask the question. But I ask it. I have to. "What are you thinking about?"

HOWARD: Here's what I was thinking: *I really, really purple her.* And here's what I said: "You."

5

BETWEEN A WOMAN AND HER CRAZY

AND THE ART OF THE SILENT MAN

Jenny got mad at me because I had an affair.

In her dream.

Yup. I was held responsible for my actions *in her subconscious.* And what's interesting is not that she admitted this was insane—she didn't—but that she told me that this had happened before. Apparently, her ex-husband cheated on her in a dream, too. And boy did he pay the price for it the next morning. Oddly, she assured me that she got much madder at him for his phantom affair than at me for mine. That made me feel better. Sort of. The good thing, she said, was that she made herself wake up from this nightmare in the middle of it, so she could be angry at me in person and we could "deal with it together." "Why didn't you just yell at me in the dream?" I asked. She preferred to yell at me in real life.

That's a pretty big wedge of crazy cheese before I even get out of the bed.

But here's what she asked me the night before as we climbed *into* bed:

"If I turned into a giant pecan pie right now, and you had to lie next to me all night, and then in the morning I would turn back into me—unless you ate me—would you not eat me?"

This took a moment to digest—so to speak. But then I calmly told her that if her life depended on it I would not eat a pecan pie. Here's what I didn't do: I did not *engage* her in a discussion. I did not say, "Can I heat you up and smother you in a giant dollop of vanilla ice cream?" Nor did I say, "What's this really about, baby?" I simply told her I would not eat pie if it meant her demise and then turned over and went to sleep.

If I'd only done that the day before . . .

I knew on the way home from work that day it was going to be a rough night. I'd gotten a text earlier in the day from her: **I'm upset that Kimmel and Silverman broke up . . . what does that mean for us?** The talented comedians and couple Jimmy Kimmel and Sarah Silverman had broken up that day. Actually, I'd read something about it three days earlier. I just hadn't told her because I knew how upset she was going to be. Jenny takes celebrity breakups very hard. Often harder than the celebrities who are doing the actual breaking up. You know how when you first break up with someone, you get that glorious day or two where you feel free and like you have a new lease on life, before the paralyzing loneliness sets in? Jenny doesn't get that day when celebrities break up. She goes right to the heartbreak. (She gets so depressed that I live in fear that the Closer and Footloose will one day call it quits.) *"What does this mean for us?"* she asked. For me, it meant it was going to be a long night.

Jimmy Kimmel and Sarah Silverman ending their relationship was a particularly bitter pill for Jenny to swallow. (Not that we know them personally or that our lives are directly affected in any way by them.) In Jenny's quest for "proof out there" that happily-ever-after exists, she had pinned high hopes on those two. And unlike, say, Top Gun and Dawson's Creek, Jimmy and Sarah were much more like us. She's offbeat and sexy-funny like Jenny. And he's funny and dumpy like me. So naturally, in her mind, if Jimmy and Sarah can't make it, neither can we. It's the transitive law of relationships:

A = B = C.

Jimmy and Sarah = Doomed Love
Howard and Jenny = Jimmy and Sarah
Howard and Jenny = Doomed Love

Here's how I feel about this way of predicting our future: It's completely nuts! But this is how her head works. Wait, it gets nuttier. Let's also factor into the crazy mix that Jenny takes television characters very seriously. *She thinks Meredith and Mc-Dreamy are real people.* And that their struggles are our struggles. She actually came up to me one night and whacked me in the chest, *hard,* because Andrew McCarthy's character, Joe Bennett, on a show called *Lipstick Jungle* had an affair with a chick who wasn't his girlfriend, Victory. She was crazy angry. "He was such a great guy! Oh HOWWWWARRRRRD!" she wailed, apparently mistaking me for Andrew McCarthy. (Like I've even seen the dude since *Weekend at Bernie's*.)[1]

So last night while lamenting the sad fate of Jimmy Kimmel and Sarah Silverman, she devolved into comparing us to other doomed television couples. Suddenly, we're Ross and Rachel, season three—when Ross thought they were "on a break" so he had sex with some ho-bag. She's Carrie to my Mr. Big when he returns from Paris engaged to a younger, hotter chick. When she compares us to Luke and Laura, "the early years," and tells me that my "anger issues" are pushing her back to Scott, I know it's time for an intervention.

Now, I know as well as anyone to not stick my toe in the crazy pool. *But I couldn't resist.* So I calmly explained to her that these characters are, in fact, not real people. I even pointed out, with cunningly cool logic I thought, that *we* of all people, who actually *write for television*, should know that Meredith and McDreamy, Ross and Rachel, and Luke and Laura aren't *even* as real as Jimmy and Sarah, let alone Howard and Jenny! It's a pretty winnable argument, right? I mean, how can you not feel you're on the right side of that one? It's a no-brainer. It's over and done with before it's even begun. I'm on terra firma with this one for sure. You'd even bet money on a stupid head like me making this point stick.

And you would lose your money.

---

[1] Several months after this incident, I e-mailed Jenny with the unfortunate news I'd just read that *Lipstick Jungle* was being canceled. Her e-mail response: **what?! oh crap . . . victory and joe bennett better get engaged then in my remaining episodes . . . are they yanking it immediately? i just want joe bennett and victory to find each other and be happy . . . (he's a billionaire and she's really skinny, if they can't find happiness then no one can!)**

A few weeks later *Lipstick Jungle* was magically uncanceled, so I guess Jenny wasn't the only one rooting for Joe Bennett and Victory.

I lost the argument. And the sad part is it wasn't even close. She blew me out of the water. She said right at the outset that I was dead wrong: Meredith and McDreamy *are* real. She then told me, "These stories come from somewhere. And they're written by real people, and if the stuff wasn't real in some way they couldn't have written it. *You* know how the writers' room works." She said almost accusingly, "Everyone shares their personal histories and that stuff ends up in the scripts!" She then reminded me, with a wink and nod, that *we* worked together "in the room" and "*we* both know how it works."

Then she brought up the specifics of some of the things I've written for television—much of it embarrassing and much of it true. But that's not all! Then she went over all the stuff that I've written that didn't really happen to me *"but it really kinda did."* And she was presenting a complex argument, because it involved the *real feelings* one has when one writes something and all the very real things I must have been thinking about at the time—which she says just bolsters her point that there's much truth in what is written, *especially when it's good.*

And suddenly, she had me believing that Meredith and McDreamy *are* real people and that their ups and downs have the power to foreshadow our own. But what's even worse is that instead of being the voice of reason—which I could have been just by ignoring her and saying nothing—*I had now validated her insane feelings.* I was sucked into the crazy vortex. I was trapped by her voodoo logic. And in this new world where right is wrong there was sure to be hell to pay. Because now she was even more unhappy, because she'd "been right all along!" And now, her worst fears confirmed, she spiraled further and further out of control. Now she was going to do things like accuse me of having an affair while I slept and wonder if I'd eat her if she was a pecan pie. I've actually managed to *increase the crazy*.

And I should have known better.

THE LESSONS OF ELIZABETH—PART TWO

EVERYTHING I KNOW ABOUT WOMEN I LEARNED AS A FRESHMAN IN COLLEGE

Yes, Elizabeth. She's baaack. Bringing all of my freshman-year denseness with her. If you want to look at your patterns of behavior with the opposite sex—and let's be honest, you probably don't—you can never go wrong by going back to that first time you really fell in love. All the mistakes to come were made then. Unfortunately, we're all too stupid in love or crazy in love to learn much from it—*then*.

With Elizabeth I definitely had all the wrong moves. But with just a little insight into how a woman's mind works, I still might have rallied with some late-inning heroics. But on this particular day my fate was sealed. It was all written on the wall of the dining room at the residence hall one night over dinner. But the really sad part is I didn't even know it.

We were eating something the cafeteria chefs called East-West Chicken, which always struck me as odd. Is it east or is it west? How can it be both? I went on a rant about the East-West Chicken, thoroughly convinced of my own wit, but she was upset that night, something having to do with her mother. It should have been just one of those things that float by, unremarked upon in the midst of conversation, as we passed the time between the East-West Chicken and the peach cobbler.

But I engaged. First mistake. But not the fatal blow. That would come shortly thereafter.

She told me that she was mad at her mother because she decided to drop her major, and her mother was supposed to tell her father, but she hadn't told him yet. Being the true freshman I was in all aspects of life, I asked her why *she* hadn't simply told her father. She said a bit tersely, "You can't talk to the guy, it's as simple as that." Which was confusing to my young inexperienced mind because she'd often talked so lovingly about her dad and what a "hoot" he was. Then she went on a tirade against her "witch of a mother" for not having relayed her decision to her father, and now he was coming up to visit, and it was going to be a disaster, and it was all her mother's fault. "All your mother's fault?" I asked dubiously. "*Really?*" She sighed, clearly irritated, and explained: It was nothing less than her mother's *responsibility* to tell her father certain things. I said (and I was so naïve at the time your heart almost breaks for me, doesn't it?), "Don't you think it's kind of *your* responsibility to tell your father certain things? Especially things that involve *you* switching majors?"

Now the steam wasn't just coming off the East-West Chicken. "*I tell my mother. Then she tells my father. That's how it works!*"

"Oh," I said. "That's fucked up." She then shot back, "Well, that's the way it always works in my family! It's the way it's always been and always will be!" I then informed her, peering down from my high horse, that her family was "*totally dysfunctional.*" ("Dysfunctional" being a word I'd learned the night before while smoking pot with some girl from Highland Park, Illinois, who was trying to convince me it was the same thing as being from Chicago.)

Now I don't remember exactly what happened next, but I'm pretty sure it involved peach cobbler being slammed down on the table and someone walking away. If memory serves, it was *she* who walked away and *me* who was the one left sitting with globs of cobbler on my shirt.

What definitely did not happen was us hooking up—which I'd still held out hope for right up until the cobbler. And remember: I LOVED HER. I WAS HEAD-OVER-HEELS FOR HER. I WAS OBSESSED WITH HER. I WOULD HAVE DONE ANYTHING FOR HER. SO WHY DIDN'T I JUST SHUT THE HELL UP?

FRESHMAN MISTAKES

I *encouraged* her to talk about a situation with her mother. Which is always a mistake. But if you do find yourself in a conversation with a chick about her mother, at the very least, *agree with her.* Just agree! No questions asked. What good can ever come from discussing the craziness of her family? The answer is none. Sympathetic nods, yes. Agreeing grunts accompanied by other eating noises, definitely. But why poke the crazy bear? And who am I to poke? Like I didn't have my own fair share of dysfunction in my family? (Whether it was her responsibility to tell her father or her mother's is quite irrelevant. I'm not sure it's the best plan to this day, but hell, if it isn't, I'm sure she's found that out on her own, thank you very much.) I painted myself into an unenviable corner. Instead of Cool Guy I Can Really Talk To, I was now Unsupportive Asshole Guy, Judgmental Jerk Guy, and the worst of all, Siding with Her Mother Guy.

I made this mistake over and over again in college. I guess everyone's family seemed so distant and strange to me and somehow so . . . *wrong.* Every girl I met seemed to come from a family that was crazier than the last one. And they all had this weird notion that it was all normal. Only my family was normal, I thought! I was so young . . . If only I'd just kept my thoughts to myself I could have had a decent freshman year.

On the first day of sophomore year I was walking down the street when my heart sank. *Elizabeth was walking hand-in-hand with a friend of mine.* In fact, I'd introduced them! I wanted to run somewhere and puke. Instead we all greeted each other with horribly strained smiles, wishing the moment would end quickly. I'd been madly in love with her for a year and he ended up getting her. After a few weeks of tension between us I made up with my friend but I never really talked to Elizabeth again. It was just too painful. After college, I lost touch with both of them. But years later, I found my friend again in Los Angeles. He and Elizabeth had long since broken up, and I asked him how he dealt with what seemed to me not only an anger at her father, but a real anger issue with men in general. He said simply, "Oh, I just shut up. What good can come from fighting that battle?"

The lessons of Elizabeth are plentiful. Not the least of which is the basic notion of having compassion for everyone. Have a big heart. Be generous with not only your love but with your forgiveness for human frailty—or insanity. We're all demented. I may not have understood this in college. But I get it now. Elizabeth was a great chick. She had some issues, but who doesn't? And wherever she is today I'm sure she's leading a fantastic, passionate, creative life.

But the more pressing lesson of Elizabeth is *don't ever get between a woman and her crazy.*

Much of the art of dealing with women is simply *getting out of the way.* Ninety percent of a successful relationship is knowing when to shut up. Women elicit your opinion but they never really want it. They just want you to be silent while they vent about you *not* giving it. Why else would they dismiss our opinion so quickly when we *do* give it? What they most certainly *do not* want is you to get all up in their business about their crazy. They want you to let their crazy breathe.

Don't ever get between a woman and her crazy.

It's a battle you can't ever win. Crazy is stronger than reason any day of the week. You wouldn't step in front of an oncoming train. So why would you get between a woman and her crazy? Unfortunately, most men labor under the false impression that it's our job to *correct* crazy. We honestly wonder how the world will ever be right if we let crazy go unabated. And if we can stop it in its tracks, we think, it will somehow make things whole in the universe. (It's really just a way of muscling a woman into thinking the exact way we do.)

But here's what my friend from college knows about crazy that you don't: **CRAZY BURNS ITSELF OUT.** You cannot douse the crazy flame. Like many a great forest fire, you let it burn out, and burn out it will. But not if you fan the flames.

THE ART OF THE SILENT MAN

The old-fashioned "strong silent type" of man often gets a bad rap from women these days. Perhaps it's too much like her distant father, but the Clint Eastwood/spaghetti Western archetype is now often thought to be a man somehow *too* distant. If not completely shut down emotionally, he's certainly lacking in the language of feelings and the ability to communicate with her meaningfully. And it's true that his stubborn reticence, especially in times of great emotional need, can add to a woman's crazy. So he's no longer most women's ideal vision of manliness or the ideal mate.

But one thing the strong silent type can teach us all is very valuable: when the hell to shut up. The strong silent type never gets between a woman and her crazy. He's keenly aware of the Mark Twain dictum "It is better to keep your mouth closed and let people think you're stupid, than to open it and remove all doubt."

Admittedly, I'm no one's idea of the silent type. I'm chatty. I can talk a blue streak. And women always find this to be a "refreshing change," especially compared to their last boyfriend. Until that first moment when I say the thing I never should have said, and they start thinking wistfully about the "uncommunicative asshole." I've stuck my foot in my mouth so many times I've had to acquire a taste for feet. I've seen words I've said turn into animated boomerangs, and in trying desperately to dodge them as they soared back at me, I only managed to make things worse. Once, as I devolved into a sputtering lunatic trying to dig myself out of another mess, Jenny warned, "Put down the shovel and move away from the hole." Which was quickly followed up by the more direct plea: *Why are you still talking?!*

So what's wrong with me and others like me? Why don't we just shut the hell up? Why have we not only gotten *between* a woman and her crazy, but *incited* her crazy?

Because we actually had something to say that wasn't stupid.

What further complicates this "Why didn't I just shut up?" thing is that often a man will have something *valid* to say. Something that's important. Something that should be said to his woman. Something that *should be* discussed in their relationship.

It's at this point that he's sure to say it at the wrong time.

When I think of some of the inopportune times I've brought things up . . . Just the stuff I've said in bed alone! Silence may not always be golden, but it sure would have been golden *then*. I may be the king of saying it at the wrong time, but I'm hardly alone. Women complain about this in men all the time: Why did the idiot have to bring it up *then*? If we'd just had some early education in *when* to say stuff, maybe we could have prevented some major bad-timing disasters. If there had just been a "Right Time to Say It" class in high school, with pop quizzes like "Now or *not* now?" maybe high school wouldn't have been such a colossal waste of time.

1. Her mother's coming in twenty minutes—NOW OR NOT NOW?
2. She's just had her hair done—NOW OR NOT NOW?
3. She just lost her job—NOW OR NOT NOW?
4. She's just blown you—NOW OR NOT NOW?
5. She wants to talk about the relationship and your inner-most feelings, even the ones that may be hurtful to her—NOW OR NOT NOW?

I think the answers to 1 through 4 are NOT NOW and the answer to 5 is NOW. Of course I'm not really sure because in my high school they were too busy teaching me useless stuff like math!

But even if you can learn these basics, you still have to learn how to *not say anything* in the heat of the moment of her craziness. Especially when that moment is blisteringly hot and even more especially when her craziness is turned directly on you.

THE FARMERS MARKET INCIDENT (AND THE GOLDEN MOMENT)

Jenny blamed me for the Santa Monica Farmers Market.

Not for there *being* a Santa Monica Farmers Market. But for her miserable experience there and for sending her there in the first place. Apparently, I should have warned her that it would be insanely crowded at that time of the morning and a parking nightmare. I know how she feels about parking and crowds—she told me—so it was downright criminal for me to let her go there.

Honestly, it was like I'd sent her to Vietnam. And she was infuriated with me. Earlier, she'd told me that she wanted to buy some fresh fruit. I didn't ask her to go buy fruit. Sure, I like fresh fruit, but I did not say to her, "I want fresh fruit, woman, and you must deliver it to me!" She asked me to recommend a farmers market and I immediately thought of the Santa Monica Farmers Market, *being that we live in Santa Monica.*

But when she came home she started raging at me. Feeling unfairly attacked, I probably would have gotten into it with her in the moment—and further incensed the crazy. Luckily, I didn't really have time because I was scheduled to go work out. And work out I did. But as I was lifting weights I started getting more and more angry. Now I was "wicked pissed," as they say in Boston. I couldn't believe she was blaming me for sending her to a place she asked me to send her to! And isn't it just common knowledge that farmers markets can be crowded sometimes!? Especially on Sundays?! If anything, I should have been hailed as a hero for answering the call, for finding fruit for a person so obviously in need of it! But all I got was grief. No good deed goes unpunished. When I finished working out, I declared to myself that I was going to give her a piece of my mind!

I went upstairs to look for her. The door to the room we call the library was closed. She never closes the door to the library. Obviously, she was still pissed and sulking. I knocked on the door. She didn't hear me or was ignoring me. My blood pressure rose as I knocked harder. *Maybe I should just knock this thing down!* And I started to "monologue" in my head: *You know what? Screw you and your anger! I'm sick of you blaming me for everything that's wrong in your life! I'm the best thing that ever happened to you, so either wake up and realize it or I'm out of here!*

Then I heard the door unlock from the other side.

And in that exact moment I remembered the other lesson of Elizabeth: *compassion.*

I slowly opened the door and peeked my head in. She was sitting on the chair looking either contrite or homicidal. I wasn't sure yet. "Are you all right? I'm concerned about you," I said. She looked up at me, eyes welling with either tears or rage. I wasn't sure yet. "Baby, I'm sorry I sent you into that nightmare," I said. "I know you hate crowds. I just wasn't thinking. The idea of having fresh peaches just blinded me I guess. I'm sorry it was a terrible experience for you. And I'm *especially sorry* that I caused it. Because I never want to intentionally cause you stress. I love you. And it's killing me, too, because it could have been avoided. I could have recommended the Palisades Farmers Market, where they have parking for three dollars, and the rich tightwads in the Palisades don't want to pay it, so there's always plenty of parking! And it's not that much further than the stupid Santa Monica Farmers Market. I'm sorry. I failed you. And I'm going to try like hell to never let that happen again."

She melted.

Then she apologized for going all bat-shit crazy on me. And five minutes later the whole thing was forgotten; we were laughing, gazing into each other's eyes lovingly, and eating fresh peaches. But I couldn't help thinking, *Oh god, what would have happened if I'd knocked the door down?!*

I'd probably be nursing a black eye from a flying peach. Or worse.

And there was a time when I definitely would have knocked that door down.

I'd like to now apologize to all those women who were on the other side of that door all those times I knocked it down. And for all those times I placed my stupid smack-dab in between a woman and her crazy in a misguided attempt to make things better, while only managing to make them worse.

Ever wonder why chicks really dig firemen? (It's not just because they're all hunky, because they're not.)

Women love a man who puts out a fire.

JENNY'S RESPONSE

BE BRIGHT, DON'T INCITE

She's already feeling emotional (what you call "crazy"). Here's how to not make it worse (what you call "crazier"):

1. **She is feeling embarrassed or humiliated.** (Example: She is dressed up and broke her heel, causing her to trip and fall in front of strangers and ruin one of her favorite pairs of shoes.)

Do NOT do any of the following:

a) Say, "Don't worry, hon, I caught the whole thing on my cell phone and you are going to be the newest star on YouTube."

b) Say, "You know I always thought those shoes were an accident waiting to happen."

c) Not help pick her up.

d) Laugh.

e) Write about it later to further embarrass her and then get the facts wrong. (Example: It was not me who wanted the fruit from the Santa Monica Farmers Market that day! I was getting the fruit *for him*! I'm not the one who needs to buy fruit with other liberals!)

2. She is feeling angry over something that IS your fault.

Do NOT do any of the following:

a) Bring up past times when she made you angry in a similar fashion.

b) Get angry back and yell at her.

c) Blame another: your kids, the dog, an innocent bystander.

d) Say, "I don't know if this level of anger is warranted here because when you think about it, it's really not that big of a deal. Don't you think you might be overreacting just a little bit?"

e) Say, "What do you want me to do? Because I've already apologized four hundred times." (This was at the end of one of our earliest fights. I say the end because after he said that I went totally ballistic on him and proceeded to scream, "*Really? That's great, good to know that all I get is four hundred apologies! I wonder how many 'I forgive you's you have left? I better go check my ledger.*")

3. She is feeling on the verge of a nervous breakdown.

(Reason: unknown. But it is obvious from one of the following signs: She is wearing pajamas or any other elastic-waistbanded pants in the late afternoon; there are empty pizza boxes, doughnut boxes, or candy wrappers that she hasn't even bothered to hide lying around; there are little wads of used Kleenex surrounding her on the floor or the couch; she's intently watching *Steel Magnolias*, *Terms of Endearment*, *Pretty Woman*, or *Practical Magic*.)

Do NOT say any of the following:

a) "I hope you saved some pizza for me."

b) "Uh, I guess Aunt Flo and her husband Morty Crampelstein have come to town."

c) "If you think you had a bad day, wait till I tell you about mine."

d) "I hope this isn't about me, because I didn't do anything."

e) "You're watching this movie again? You do know she dies, right?"

4. She is sick in bed.

Do NOT say any of the following:

a) "Whatever you do, don't give it to me."

b) "Wow, you look terrible."

c) "The only one who has a nose redder than yours is a drunk or that reindeer, what's his name? You know, the one with the red nose. What's his name? C'mon, you know his name. God, it's gonna drive me crazy till I think of it. Will you Google and tell me? I'm dying here."

d) "I would make you pancakes or soup but I don't know how."

e) "I would make you pancakes or soup but I know how you hate it when I mess up the kitchen."

f) "I would make you pancakes or soup but you know how I'm trying not to eat pancakes these days." (This one is classic Howard.)

5. She is feeling sad and depressed.

Do NOT do any of the following:

a) Try to joke her into cheering up. Meaning: Do not shoot her with Silly String, do not plastic-wrap the toilet like you used to do in camp, and do not push up the sides of her mouth and say, "Someone needs to turn that frown upside down."

b) Try to make her feel better with the relativity approach. "Babe, it's all relative. I mean, you *do* know there are people out there who have it much worse than you. Here, let me go and get the globe and I'll show you the countries they're in."

c) Talk about the fact that you never really "got" depression until you saw that commercial with the sad cartoon circle that was depressed and didn't bounce very high but that later went on meds and appeared much happier. And don't say, "Are you feeling like that sad cartoon circle?"

d) Say, "Whassa matter baby?" in an exaggerated baby voice and then proceed to get in bed with her and start baby-talking up a storm or mock-crying.

e) Do that thing where you (Howard) pretend to crack an egg on her head with your hands and then simulate it oozing down the front of her face. (It will, as we've seen, only make her start to cry.)

6. She is feeling admittedly crazy, irrational, hysterical, etc.

Do NOT do any of the following:

a) Try to reason with her.

b) Say, "You are acting crazy!" or "You are acting irrational!" (Trust me, we know.)

c) Start talking in a weird and what you think is a "soothing TV therapist type" voice.

d) Talk to her like a she's a rabid animal, deaf, or stupid.

e) Just passively climb on board the crazy train.

f) Make it about yourself in any way. She called dibs on the crazy, and it's up to you to help her in any way that is most helpful to her.

And when in doubt about any scenario, you really can't go wrong with hugging her, cuddling her, trying to make her laugh (but not at her expense, please!), and telling her that you love her no matter how she's feeling. And if you make pancakes or cook soup, just make sure to clean up the kitchen afterward.

Trust me, it's not as hard to deal with the crazy as you might think. Just figure out what *she* needs and do it for *her*. And if you need it even more simplified: SUSS AND FUSS. First, you suss out her emotional state (i.e., is she feeling fat? Really fat? Cranky? Sulky? Pouty? Pissy?) and then make a fuss over her (flowers, pancakes, balloons, or jewelry)!

6

SIGN LANGUAGE

This year we had a boring, miserable Labor Day. I was up all night before with a bad stomach watching the Jerry Lewis telethon. (Gloria Gaynor is still surviving after all these years!) Jenny was tired and coming down with a throat infection. We had big plans that were scaled back, then canceled altogether when our washing machine flooded and water came gushing down the stairs. (It's on the top floor; don't ask.) We ended up walking to Blockbuster in the blistering heat with our dog, about to get her own miserable infection, where we rented a horror movie called *Prom Night*. (Jenny's pick; she likes scary movies.) If it's not the worst movie ever made, it's close. And as we prayed for night to release us from the long wait to go to bed, an all too familiar look came over Jenny's face. And I knew what was coming. I'd heard it so many times before . . .

"What if it's a sign?"

As we've seen in my last chapter, Jenny tends to put a lot of meaning onto things that may or may not have any meaning at all for us. "It's a sign!" she often says to me. But even more often, *"What if it's a sign?"* And this question can come off of anything I do. Or anything at all. Most often it's a comparison to what I did previously in the relationship. And the fact that I *used to* and *don't anymore* always means the same thing: *"It's a sign."*

And bad signs always trump good signs.

We had a great time on the day before our lousy Labor Day. But whatever "sign" came from having a great day *before* Labor Day was immediately cast aside by the obviously more potent sign of having a miserable Labor Day. I had also called her a while ago and told her to go to the *People* magazine website, which had the big headline JIMMY KIMMEL AND SARAH SIL-VERMAN ARE BACK ON! The article went on to say, "They're taking it slow, but they're on the road back to being together again." "That has to be a good sign!" I yelled into the phone. "Or at least a reversal of a bad sign, right?"[1]

"I guess . . . ," was her surprisingly flat response. "But now I'm worried about Téa Leoni and David Duchovny," she said. He'd checked himself into a rehab clinic for sexual addiction. Several months later they announced they were getting separated. Turns out that *was* a bad sign.

But the search for signs in relationships, real or otherwise, is hardly unique to Jenny. It's a preoccupation with all women. Partially because the search for meaning in all things is their nature, but it's also the natural result of men being less than forthcoming about their feelings—even the good ones. That leaves a lot of room for a woman's active imagination to grow,

---

[1] As this book went to pubication, Sarah Silverman and Jimmy Kimmel broke up again, proving once and for all the danger of using celebrities' relationships as "signs" for our own. Frankly, I can't take the roller coaster that is Jimmy and Sarah anymore.

a lot of room for *interpretation,* and a lot of room for *signs.* A woman's mind is a dangerous thing. And musings left to their own devices can quickly escalate out of control.

Men, on the other hand, tend to assume everything's fine and go along with their business until they come home to find their wives are leaving them. *"Whuh?"* we say. *"I never saw the signs!"* Ever talk to a recently divorced couple? Chances are, she's bitter and he's confused. (He gets bitter later. But confusion always comes first.) She'd sent out signs for months that she was truly unhappy but he'd been blissfully ignorant. Men tend only to see signs in retrospect, which isn't very effective sign seeing.

Women see signs everywhere. (CRAZY.)

Men *miss* signs everywhere. (STUPID.)

SIGNS OF SEX

Here's what else didn't happen on Labor Day: We didn't have sex.

Somewhere between me running to the bathroom, Jenny having another coughing fit, us both getting more towels and buckets to fend off the water rapidly filling up our house, and both of us generally feeling tired, depressed, and irritated, we didn't have all that much zest to do it.

But it was a holiday, I was told, and once you stop having "holiday sex" it's a sign of something really bad.

Sex is full of signs. No aspect of a relationship is more rife with obsessing over signs and their possible meaning than what he or she did or didn't do in bed. And it's a particularly loaded subject because of the way sex changes over the course of a relationship. First there's lots and lots of it. And then less. And then not so much.

This freaks us all out.

Because we were positive it would be different this time. The therapists all tell us that it's normal for a sex life to wane and be replaced by a softer, cuddlier version of love. Sex in a long-term relationship, they assure us, ebbs and flows. But most people's experience is that when it ebbs it doesn't flow back. So signs run rampant on both sides as we guard against, or *gird for*, the inevitable slowdown of what was once a fervent passion. The moment when she tells her girlfriends, "He didn't do the thing!" or he insists, "She used to *love to,* I swear!"

I know a man who always took his watch off before sex so as to not scratch his girlfriend's skin. She found this to be a stunningly good sign of his sensitivity to her skin and by extension to her feelings. Then came the inevitable night when he left it on. It was a sign, she thought, and not a good one. I know a woman who shared a great love of sports with her boyfriend. Then one night he suggested they have sex *while watching SportsCenter.* And yet at the time, she didn't see this as a sign that maybe this wasn't going to be the most romantic and intimate of relationships. She should have.

IT *IS* A SIGN

Sometimes signs are signs and sometimes they're not. Women err on the side of seeing too many false signs—which makes them crazy. And men err by never seeing any at all—which makes them stupid. However, understanding the difference between real and false signs is often tremendously difficult.

Freud, the master of interpreting signs, said, "Sometimes a cigar is just a cigar." Except when it isn't.

I'm not too proud to tell you that there are a few signs I missed along the way. First marriages are chock-full of signs to be missed, ignored, and then later argued about and regretted. For my thirty-sixth birthday, my ex-wife surprised me with a trip to San Francisco, where we stayed at the beautiful Sherman House. I awoke the next morning to find that many of my close friends had flown up to attend a surprise birthday party for me that night on a chartered boat in San Francisco Bay, where we had a sumptuous catered dinner and then I was showered with presents and love. Oh, and that night there just happened to be a huge fireworks display over the bay, so we had the best seats in the house without any of the hassle of having to deal with the crowds.

To review: Boat, catered dinner, fruity drinks, great friends, presents, and abundant love all around.

The next year she got me a walking stick.

A walking stick.

Like a thing that you . . . *walk with.*

She explained it was a Navajo walking stick and it did have a decorative handle. But basically it was a stick you might find on a walk. You'd pick up the stick. And you'd walk with it for the duration of the walk, and then you'd discard it because *it's a fucking stick.* By the way, I'm not much of a walker. I don't particularly enjoy walking. I don't seek it out as a preferred activity. If I have to get off my ass to, say, go to the car, I'm fine with it. Other than that, not a fan of walking.

Yet this was my birthday present from my wife.

Welcome to thirty-seven. Here's a stick.

She was essentially telling me to walk and to *keep walking*.

By my thirty-eighth birthday I was having dim sum with a few friends and no wife on a Sunday afternoon. My wife was too busy becoming my ex-wife.

And yet I never saw the signs. There were many, many signs leading up to the Stick. And I missed all of them. But women, especially women in love, are not immune to missing signs either. And my ex-wife missed a sign or two. For instance:

I threw her in front of a deer once.

In retrospect that was a sign too.

And she missed it completely!

I mean, she didn't miss that I was throwing her in front of the deer, as she was helplessly hurtling toward it. She got that. But she wrote it off at the time as me being a scared "city kid" deeply uncomfortable with the wild outdoors—even though I grew up in the same suburb of Boston as she did. We were at a beautiful resort in Big Sur. Neither of us could sleep, so we decided to head outside to soak ourselves in the infinity hot tub nestled into the side of a cliff overlooking stunning Northern California vistas. As we were emerging from our luxury cabin in our velvety-soft terry-cloth robes, a fawn jumped out in front of us.

Yes, a fawn. Not even a deer. A little doe. As in "doe, a deer."

And I just reacted! Not well, obviously. In seeking protection from this creature in the night I instinctively shoved her in front of me. To be fair, she was always much more outdoorsy than me. And in fact she didn't panic at all. Bambi, on the other hand, bolted for the hills. Upon being told later that deer come out at night, and that they're more easily scared than people, and that the last thing this fawn was going to do was attack, I said, "How am I supposed to know this?! What am I, a park ranger?"

This was a sign.

And not just a sign that I'm the last guy you want to go on a camping trip with. There was something else in my action, however rash and reactive it was. It signaled some bit of truth that haunted our relationship. An unwillingness perhaps, on my part, to sacrifice for her, to fully give myself to that relationship in the way a man does when he instinctively throws himself in front of a bullet for a truly loved one.

Or stands in front of a little fawn at a fancy resort.

She might not have been troubled at the time, but she filed the sign away in her subconscious. In the waning days of our marriage, she accused me in counseling of always putting myself first and looking out for me at a cost to her. When I protested, she screamed, *"You threw me in front of a deer!"*

Hard to get happy after that one.

I tell you this, mortifying as it is, to point out that no one is immune from missing the signs. And love will mess you up every time. Love obscures the signs we should see clearly as it simultaneously highlights the meaningless signs we should just ignore. That's messed up! And everyone is vulnerable to it. The challenge of any relationship is in *how we tell the signs apart.* How we see the signs that are real for what they are—and discard the rest. If Jenny sees a raven in the middle of the road she's stressed out for a week. (She once broke off an engagement over such a thing!) But I'm talking about signs in people's behavior, in what they do, or don't do, that should give us all a clue as to how they'll act in the future. I've seen too many stupid men not understand why their woman left them (me included) despite signs so ominous and potent they practically tripped over them on the way to the can. I've also seen too many crazy chicks trying to read the tea leaves in a cup of coffee—driven to the brink by their own dark take on a benign or even loving act.

Sometimes a bad Labor Day is just a bad Labor Day.

Unless somebody's throwing somebody in front of a deer.

Since the failure of my marriage, I've tried to hone my sign-seeing skills—with various degrees of success. In a relationship after my divorce, a woman told me that she was okay *not* having kids, which was fine with me, since I don't feel about kids as I do about potato chips—you *can* just have one. Actually, she *might* want them, she said; she didn't really know. I mean, yes, she wanted the option, and she was definitely in those prime babymaking years, and all of her friends seemed to be having them, but still, their path wasn't necessarily her path. All in all, she was pretty sure she was okay with not having a kid.

But I noticed that quite often when she took her birth control pill she dropped it. Somewhere on the way from her hand to her mouth it was fumbled. And as she was exasperatedly searching for it on the floor, she said, "I don't know why this always happens! It's probably because they're so small!"

That sign I picked up on.

FIRST-DATE SIGNS

The signs at the very beginning of a relationship are really the only ones that have any practical value for us to take note of. All the rest come when it's already too late. And people have a subtle way of revealing themselves on a first date—which in retrospect is never subtle. One need only pay attention. Unfortunately, one rarely does.

On a first date, a woman assured me she was "totally over" her longtime boyfriend, and then proceeded to talk about him for much of the night. A clear sign. But did I heed that warning? Of course not. She was gorgeous and really smart. (I gleaned the smart part from the precious few moments when I managed to get her off the subject of her supposed ex.) We had some great nonboyfriend talks on the phone after, and I started to get my hopes up. Then of course the phone calls stopped and it wasn't long before I heard she was back with the guy. *And yet, I still managed to be surprised at this development.*

Another woman openly admitted that she was "flaky" on our first date. But she said that people mistook her flakiness for not caring. And that wasn't true, she assured me. She cared deeply about people. Especially the people she got involved with. She wanted me to know that. On our first date. Which went extremely well. Later of course she completely flaked out on me and I went nuts. How could she do this? Things were going so well! Late one night some months later she called to apologize for "flaking out" but reminded me of what she'd said when we first met. It was cold comfort. But it was comfort of a sort.

On another first date the subject of therapy came up. And, perhaps revealing too much, I told the woman about all the money I'd spent on it over the years, but how I didn't really mind because essentially therapy was my hobby. She immediately said she didn't approve of all this therapy stuff and that it seemed to her to be "soooo self-indulgent." The next night she called me to tell me she felt terrible about impugning my one hobby and that she didn't *really* think I was self-indulgent. But I'd already concluded that it was a bad sign.

I've done my own share of posting up signs on first dates.

On my first date with Jenny, I apparently told her that I have a tendency to wear down women. I don't remember telling her this, but it sure does sound like me. (First I wear out their resistance and then, once I have them, I wear out their patience.) I'm a difficult man, no doubt. Just wanted her to know.

Turns out she already knew.

But if everyone is consciously or unconsciously revealing themselves from the very beginning, why do we so often miss even the clearest of signs?

Because love will mess you up every time.

Or the *possibility* of love.

Or the possibility of sex.

Women tend to lose their sanity over signs of love, while men tend to act stupider than normal over signs of sex. What else is new? (If the more important of a man's two brains is being satisfied, pretty much everything else is cool with him. *What signs? She wanted to do it!*) But the desperate bestowing of meaning on signs by both sides later in a relationship is just the inevitable result of all the missed signs we should have seen at the start.

THE WORST FIRST-DATE SIGN EVER MISSED

On Woody Allen and Mia Farrow's first date he told her, "I have zero interest in children." And he explained how he avoided his own sister, whom he loved dearly, because he couldn't stand being around her kids. But still, Mia thought to herself, *he doesn't really mean it.* Who could really hate children? Especially someone so brilliant and funny and sensitive as Woody Allen. I bet he'd be wonderful around children!

This was a sign she should have heeded.

He told a woman with seemingly six hundred kids he had *ZERO INTEREST* in children. Not even 1 or 2 percent. Zero. This was an unbelievably overt sign. There's not a lot of wiggle room in "zero percent." She actually had seven kids at the time, with plans to adopt more. Could a red flag be any redder? But Mia didn't see it. Ironically, it turned out Woody Allen actually did have some interest in children. As we all know, he started sleeping with Mia's daughter Soon-Yi— who was twenty-two at the time. (But to be fair, they had a long history. He'd known her *since she was eight.*) When pressed later for an explanation for this act, he famously told *Time* magazine, "The heart wants what it wants."

Which was really just a sign that he's an asshole.

TO HEED OR NOT TO HEED: THAT IS THE QUESTION

The first time I noticed Jenny Lee, I mean, *really* noticed her, in that way that makes one sit up and say, "Wait a minute, what's this?" she was wearing an orange bathing suit and a bright orange Cookie Monster T-shirt. She was playing in the pool with my son and some other kids at a pool party for people we worked with. She was this bright orange wonder with great legs. She was the sun that day. And I couldn't take my eyes off her. On the way home from the party, my son asked me the name of that big girl who was playing with him. And all I kept thinking was, *Orange . . . isn't that the warning sign right before red?*

A month or so later we met for lunch on a Sunday afternoon. We'd started secretly seeing each other, and although I was falling fast, it was far from clear to either of us that dating someone you work closely with in a television writer's room was a sound idea. There were so many potential pitfalls. As we kissed good-bye in the parking lot, I noticed she was wearing a bright puffy orange ski jacket. And in my typically deft manner I blurted out, "You look like a highway cone."

She was a walking, talking warning sign come to life.

She laughed, luckily. But the image of a highway warning cone, with its promise of peril just up the road or around the bend, was not lost on either of us.

An orange warning cone indeed . . .

A week later she broke up with me.

She came over to my house, in a purple dress, having forsaken orange for a more healing color, and told me that we should just stop this whole thing before we got more involved. It was sure to lead to pain and anguish and we should cut our losses before one of us really got hurt. But I wasn't going to let her go that easily. I told her what I'd only recently realized: "Whatever you're worried about happening . . . *has already happened.*" If you're going to open your heart, it's already too late to protect it.

Here's the thing about warning signs: The only thing more crazy or more stupid than *not* heeding a warning sign *may just be heeding it.* What then? Wait another hundred years for the person with no signs attached? Better to be a fool for love than just a fool. And a lonely one at that. Signs can only protect you from so much. I mean, sure, if you hear that a guy threw his ex-wife in front of a fawn, that might give you pause. Perhaps there would be a flashing red light going off somewhere in your brain. But you might also be missing a sign that says that the guy is capable of change. Just because someone throws a woman in front of a deer *once* doesn't mean they'd do it again.

I never told her about the deer thing.

Why didn't I tell her?

I'm guessing it's a sign . . .

JENNY'S RESPONSE

IF YOU GIVE A RABID RACCOON YOUR GIRLFRIEND . . .

I'm not going to lie to you; I'm a little freaked out about the deer story. I find it odd that we are almost at our two-year anniversary mark and I have never heard this story before. Now, I'm a fairly reasonable woman and I understand that we can't possibly know everything about each other's pasts. But one thing that must be factored into the equation is that Howard and I are both very chatty people—I mean the two of us can really be classified as talkers—so given this fact, I'm pretty sure I can say that we know more about each other than most other couples after two years. Plus, I'm superinquisitive in general—Third-Degree Lee, they call me. (Not really, but I've always wanted a nickname other than Spaz, which was my nickname at camp in sixth grade.)

I'm definitely the girlfriend who wants to know every single detail about all the past girlfriends, so I know which massage oils to never buy because that was what he used with *her*. (One of Howard's earliest rookie stupid moves was that he bought us some "massage oil" that he had discovered and used with *some other girl*! And when I reacted badly to it, he's all like, "What? It's good stuff. And it's a new bottle, so I'm not saying we use the old stuff under the bathroom sink." And I'm like, "Oh, that's nice that I deserve my own fresh bottle as opposed to the almost empty bottle that is all smeary with oily fingerprints, toe prints, and whatever other kind of prints might have gotten on the bottle. But it's fine. Really. You know, I was going to buy a new pair of chocolate handcuffs for you, but now I don't have to. The pair I have only has a few bites out of it; you see, the guy I was with really didn't like milk chocolate, only dark chocolate, and so after a few bites he was like . . . eh, it's a long story, are you sure you want to know?")

Howard, not amused with my level of sarcasm, waved his hand to signal that he had had enough. He didn't even ask whether my story was true. It wasn't. (Please, you think I'd share if I had a pair of handcuffs made out of milk chocolate? Not a chance.)

What I'm trying to say is that in the two years that we'd been together, I thought we had pretty much woken up every sleeping dog in our past (woken it up, taken it out, got it groomed, bought it a new collar . . .). I mean, I figured that I had either heard about or witnessed pretty much all the big stuff. Apparently not.

Now granted, I understand that it was wildlife that he threw his ex-wife in front of as opposed to, say, an oncoming SUV, but still. And of course I feel a bit guilty even giving a moment's pause over such an incident because it shows that I am falling prey to those traditional gender roles. Like how men are supposed to be big and strong and their role is to protect their women. And how women are supposed to be weak and small and their job is to make dinner for their big strong men. But even though I don't buy into that way of thinking, I must admit, I can't help but wonder what might happen if while strolling through our neighborhood together, a pissed-off squirrel appeared in our path throwing acorns. Should I now just assume it will be up to me to protect not only myself, but him as well, from angry blackbirds, lost rhinos, and lonely wolves?

There is a series of little kids' picture books that was introduced to me by Howard's son, Dustin, that I really like. The first one is called *If You Give a Mouse a Cookie*. (The others we have are *If You Give a Pig a Pancake* and *If You Give a Moose a Muffin*.) In the beginning of the first story, a mouse is given a cookie. (Obviously, this isn't a real mouse that lives in between your walls and carries germs, has little beady eyes, and would make you stand on a chair and scream bloody murder if you saw it in your kitchen; no, this is a very friendly, darling even, hand-drawn cartoon mouse that is wearing denim overalls—or perhaps a jaunty red jacket.)

So in the beginning of the story the boy gives the mouse a cookie, and then the mouse needs some milk, and then the mouse needs a straw . . . And one thing leads to another, with the mouse eventually wrecking the whole house. These stories probably appeal to me so much because I am a big believer that one seemingly small innocent action, like, say, giving a cartoon mouse a cookie, could actually set in motion a catastrophe of epic proportions. (And let me just say that I could have told you that giving a moose a muffin would be a bad idea. Moose are really big and there is no way they are going to be able to get the muffin wrapper off with their big ol' hooves. And a frustrated moose screams trouble. But I digress.)

So armed with this newfound information about Howard's past, I start to imagine the fallout if a similar incident were to happen to us. In my head I picture Howard and me taking an evening stroll, and let's assume we are out of town, because normally when we are outside together in our own neighborhood we are with our 110-pound Newfie puppy, Doozy, who undoubtedly would scare away most wildlife in our path. So there we are walking, let's say in New York City, which is totally reasonable as we tend to go there once or twice a year. So we've just eaten this decadent meal at some little gem of a bistro in the West Village, and we're walking hand in hand on a brisk October night. Suddenly, we hear a loud clank and the corner trash can five feet away spills over and a big fat rabid raccoon spills out and belly flops onto the sidewalk—oof, right on his face. Embarrassed and mad, he springs up a few feet into the air and throws a partially eaten knish at us.

Howard, being closer to the raccoon and still holding my hand, whips me forward and to his left so that he's now hiding behind me and I'm face-to-face with the little black-eyed thug. And so the raccoon says, "Whoa, buddy, what's this? Did you just throw your girlfriend at me? Are you giving her to me?" I look at the raccoon and then back at Howard, who has an expression on his face that I can't really read, and when Howard doesn't answer, I shrug and say, "I think he is." And the raccoon says, "Great, do you think you can hail a cab and take me to the vet? I'm really not feeling well. I've got a bitch of a headache."

And I say, "Sure," and we take off, leaving Howard standing alone on the sidewalk. The story would then proceed to have Howard's night quickly begin to circle the drain until he is homeless and living in a refrigerator box in the park, all because he threw me to a raccoon like I was a used piece of tinfoil.

When I explain this scenario to Howard he tells me not only is this the silliest story he's ever heard, but that I'm wrong. He says he's different now. He explains that he believes his ex-wife missed a sign when he threw her in front of the deer, whereas with me, he was pretty sure it wouldn't have happened at all. And there was no way he was going to just hand me over to a raccoon as he has never found them to be particularly scary.

I tell him that size doesn't matter when it comes to rabies and that those little masked creatures would be hell to pick out of a lineup.

I tell him I just want to understand what exactly is going through his mind. Is this now a hypothetical situation? Is it one of those "If a tree falls in the forest . . ." type questions, except now it's "If a fawn was traipsing through the woods . . ."? Or is it that he thinks it wouldn't happen again because it's happened before and now he knows what a fawn looks like and he's sure he could take it if Bambi happened to want to throw down? Or is it that he thinks it wouldn't happen now because he and I have a very different relationship than what he had with his ex? *And if so, could he please tell me what's so different about our relationship that makes him certain he wouldn't pitch me to a panda bear if we happened to run into one?!*

Howard tells me he has no idea what I'm talking about. He always gets frustrated with the speculative "what if" scenarios that I am constantly spinning. He states that he knows it wouldn't happen again. So I ask him to clarify: Is it that it wouldn't happen to him ever again *regardless of what girl he happens to be with*? Or is it that it wouldn't happen again because of me specifically? (There's a difference, you know.) He ignores my latest query and goes so far as to promise that he wouldn't give me away to *any* woodland creature at all, and I'm reminded of that childhood saying "Pretty please, with a cherry on top, with thirty-one flavors of ice cream," and then you are asked to name the thirty-one flavors, and you do because it's part of the deal. So I ask him to name all the animals he wouldn't throw me at and he gamely names a few—zebra, antelope, rabbit, penguin—but eventually he stops because he realizes this is a dumb request on my part.

Even after this naming of the animals I can't help but ask him one more time how he can be sure. I think he senses my anxiety is coming from someplace that I can't locate, like a leak in a ceiling overhead that could be coming from any number of pipes.

He tells me he loves me and that's how he's sure.

And that's it. I feel better. I believe he is right that women are always looking for signs, but it's because we have a vested interest in the future of the relationship. The big question anytime you first start dating a guy is "Where is this relationship going?" You wonder that upon meeting a guy. Will we make it to a first date? When you're on the first date you're already wondering whether there will be a good-night kiss or even a second date. You wonder whether you'll make it to sex. You wonder when he'll tell his friends about you and when you'll have the talk that you should exclusively be seeing only each other. Women, it seems, just can't help wondering what's on down the road.

Perhaps since women's expectations for love and romance are higher than men's, we know there is more chance for disappointment, so we look to signs for comfort. Maybe women know that relationships have no blueprints or engineering specs to back them up and that sometimes even trains can derail. And if you're not sure what's happening in the relationship, because you don't know how the guy you're with feels about you, then what choice do you have but to read signs? (His mother is coming to town and he wants you to meet her; good sign. He drinks too much at parties and then hits on your friends; very bad sign.) Perhaps if men communicated their feelings more clearly women wouldn't be left to their own devices to figure out what's going on.

Big deal, so my boyfriend threw his ex-wife in front of a deer.

But he's with me now and every relationship is different, thank god. People (yes, even men) learn and grow and gain self-awareness from their mistakes (hopefully) and just because he made some major gaffe with some woman from his past doesn't mean it's going to happen to me. (Though if your boyfriend's last two girlfriends disappeared under suspicious circumstances then you might want to tread carefully.)

Yeah, so what, Howard threw his ex-wife in front of a deer.

That sign, however big and flashing it appears to be, is not actually on the side of the particular highway that Howard and I are currently traveling on together. I know I have to let it go and just believe that he has every intention of protecting me from whatever lurks outdoors. (He is excellent at killing bugs and is always gallant about coming and picking up dead flies after I kill them, and I sure find that to be a good sign.) Good. Done. Great. Phew.

. . .

I picture Howard's assistant, Heather, sitting in a Hollywood Assistants Anonymous meeting one day in the future. "Hi. I'm Heather. My boss's girlfriend asked me to find a live deer and let it loose in their path at dusk one night to see what he would do. You see, he had thrown his ex-wife in front of a deer, and he said that she should have recognized this as a sign that the relationship was in trouble, so now his new girlfriend wants to know how committed he is to her. I'm happy to report that he did not throw her in front of the deer and all is peaceful in the house!

"But if you happen to see a lost deer walking around Santa Monica it'd be great if you could call me on the number that's on the flier on the back table by the cookies. You see, I only rented the deer for a week . . ."

7

AN INCONSISTENT WOMAN . . .

. . . A CONFUSED MAN

I hugged Jenny Lee in bed the other night and this is what she said in her usual rapid-fire delivery: "I think I've lost weight, don't you? Don't say anything. Have I?"

"Uh . . . am I supposed to answer that one?"

"You are. You're not. You are."

Now all I could muster was my usual irritated and weary look.

"You're supposed to answer," she explained, "but not with too much enthusiasm. If you're like, 'Yeah, you *have* lost weight! You bet!' and say it all gleeful-like, it's basically saying, 'You *were* a fat pig.' So you should answer in a kind of dull monotone and with unexpressive eyes."

So I said it like a robot. "You. Have. Lost. Weight."

"Okay, that's terrible," she said.

"You said to do it in a monotone!"

"But you're not supposed to say, 'You have lost weight.'"

"But you told me to say you lost weight!"

"You're supposed to say, 'You look great, hon!' But just say it simply and move on."

"You look great, hon!" I said simply with great hopes of moving on.

She shook her head in disgust. "Terrible. Just terrible."

I bring this up to demonstrate just how difficult it is to have a conversation with a woman, because you're not just talking to her. You're also talking to all her contradictions. *You are. You're not. You are.* This makes "To be or not to be" seem like a model of constancy. In fact, "You are. You're not. You are" encapsulates the great predicament of every man who has ever loved a woman. One must understand the meaning of these tortured little sentences before even attempting to engage with a woman on any level. "You are. You're not. You are." So what does this really mean? It means: You're fucked. You're not. You are.

Because up is down and down is up. Often in the same second.

The other night in a new Mario Batali restaurant, I was devouring a succulent late-night pork chop when Jenny announced to me that she didn't like Las Vegas. Which was fine with me—just a little unfortunate for her because *we were in Las Vegas*. But I accepted her feelings, because hell, not everyone likes Vegas, and she's taught me the value of accepting others' feelings, and I had a pork chop to suck dry.

But then she told me that *I* wasn't having a good time, either.

And I kind of stared at her for a moment. Because I had been under the distinct impression that I *was* having a good time. And I told her so. She then informed me in no uncertain terms that I was *not* having a good time. And if I thought I was, I was lying to myself. Apparently, it was inconceivable to her that I could be having a good time if she wasn't. *"That's just inconsistent,*" she said. This from the mind that gave us "You are. You're not. You are." Well, one thing *was* for sure: I wasn't having a good time anymore.

But that wasn't the most tortured moment that I wished had stayed in Vegas. The next morning we both woke up depressed. She was into her second day of depression, and me too, apparently, although it still felt like my first. But in order to salvage this disaster of a Vegas morning, I asked her what she wanted to do that day. And truthfully, all I cared about was that she have a good day. I would have even willingly gone to an orchid show had that been her fancy. So I said cheerfully, "I'll do anything you want." To which she replied, *"That's not what I want!"*

To review: I offer to do *anything* she wants. And she says, "That's not what I want!" How can *anything she wants* not be what she wants?! It's by definition WHAT SHE WANTS! How could that not be acceptable?!

Because she's a woman. That's how.

Which brings us to today: It's a beautiful Sunday afternoon; my son has a playdate with his pal Kevin, whom he's known since he was born; and Jenny and I decided yesterday that this afternoon we'd get some work done on this book—despite our desire to see Angelina Jolie kick some ass in slow motion. But when I go upstairs to tell her I'm going to my office to write, I find her looking online at movie times and she suggests we go to one. So I tell her we have to work. She then accuses me of not thinking of her because "it's all about what *you* want." But I remember *distinctly* our previous day's conversation where it was actually *she* who'd concluded, "We'll feel bad if we don't work." So I parrot her *exact words* back to her and say, "We'll feel bad if we don't work."

But now she sighs. I'm always in trouble when she sighs.

"When you say '*We'll* feel bad' you really mean '*you'll* feel bad,'" she says.

"I'm just saying what you said to me yesterday!"

"But when I said 'we' I meant 'you,'" she explains.

"How could you mean *me* when you used the word '*we*'?"

"Because when I said 'we' I meant 'you' but when you said 'we' you *only* meant 'you.'"

"That's ridiculous! Even if it were true that I had some diabolical plan to get my way by saying 'we' every time I meant 'me,' *you were the one who said it first!*"

"Because I was looking out for you," she says. "Because I care about what *you* want."

"So you change the meaning of words?!"

"Yes. Because I love you."

To review: I was supposed to know that *because she loves me,* she changes pronouns to make me feel less alone and give voice to my self-centered desires. And because she does that for me, I was *then* supposed to know to *not* use those same words to make a point. Because they weren't really *her* words. They were in fact *my* words. Even though I didn't know they were my words and I didn't use them.

CONFUSED YET?!

WHY CAN'T A WOMAN BE MORE LIKE A MAN?

In *My Fair Lady* Rex Harrison asked this very question in his famous sing/speak style of singing. But what Rex was really asking was, "Why can't a woman be *consistent* like a man?" The nature of a woman is to be inconsistent. This is a huge problem for men. A man can count on a handful of things about his woman, yes. But even the things you can count on, you can't even count on. Men, on the other hand, are consistent to a fault. But predictability has its advantages—if not always its charms—because women can easily gain knowledge about us through our repeated behaviors. We have no such advantage with them! They're wild cards just about every time. With a women, every time is, as the method actors like to say, "as if for the first time." Which keeps things fresh, sure, but it's also like dealing with someone with Alzheimer's. What came before doesn't matter. Even a minute before! A woman can switch up on you and change her personality completely in a manner of seconds. You can take the trash out and come back to find a completely different woman from the one you left! Men are the same day in, day out—boring perhaps, monotonous even, mind-numbing in our sameness. But there's a key that fits to our lock and we've given you multiple copies of it for safekeeping.

Women are, perhaps, more complex emotionally—which they all seem to take as a good thing. (I'm not so sure.) And they are able to empathize more easily because of an innate ability to see two sides of any situation. (Even when there's only one.) But the gulf between what *is* and what *was* five minutes ago, between what is said and what is meant, and between what is seemingly agreed upon and then silently rescinded often seems too big a divide to conquer. As a man I often wonder: *How do they expect us to know what is essentially unknowable?*

And yet, they do.

IS A WOMAN KNOWABLE?

I could finish the chapter here.

I could say, "Oh, rats, this is just the way it is," and leave it up to Jenny and all the other women of the world to write their own chapters on how if we only paid a little more attention we could figure them all out. *But I'm not going to give them the satisfaction.* I will be a confused man no more. I am going to prove—or disprove, as the case may be—this romantic notion shared by inconsistent women everywhere that *if you just look hard enough* every woman is knowable, if only for a moment. In *The Last of the Mohicans* Daniel Day-Lewis shouted to Madeleine Stowe, "I will find you! No matter what occurs!" And now I shout to my woman, "I will try to find you! But what will occur?!" Wow. That's just not as cool as what he shouted.

A REAL PEONY IN MY ASS

Women like flowers, right? That's a basic concept we can all agree on. You don't often hear of a woman presented with flowers saying, "Get those sweet-smelling pretty things away from me!" Unless she's deathly allergic to them. So if, say, a man stopped off on his way home and got a woman with no allergies flowers for no particular reason other than that he loves her, that would be a good thing, right?

Not so fast.

Jenny's favorite flowers are peonies. And peony season is a very short one. (And it's never during Valentine's Day, you should note if you happen to be with a peony chick.) So a few Celtics games ago (that's how I measure time during the playoffs), Jenny said in a high whiny voice that's an acquired taste, "I want peonies! They're only in season for a short time! And you missed it last year and I really want peonies!"

Duly noted.

Now of course I couldn't get them for her the next day. Because then I'd have been accused of just getting them because she told me to. And that's not romantic. And that's not right. She wanted me to spontaneously think of my love for her—and her love of peonies—and then burst forth from whence I sat, wherever I might be, and get her those peonies because peonies suit her so. And just in case I needed help being spontaneous, she made sure to tell me the peony clock was ticking.

Oh, and one other thing: Jenny doesn't like "sorry flowers." Not flowers that are weeds or shriveled up daisies, but flowers that are presented after someone (always me) has made a big booboo and is using them to apologize. I've been told that "sorry flowers" don't count. They're accepted and in some cases appreciated by her, but they certainly don't count as a girl getting flowers from her guy. So it was important that I get this spontaneous desire to present her with flowers during peony season and not while in the doghouse.

Here's the crazy thing: I got it! It was another Sunday afternoon four or five days after her peony dictum. I was sitting at my computer and I just spontaneously thought to myself: *Jenny's great! I've been watching a lot of basketball lately and she's been very supportive. In fact, tonight I have a couple of buddies coming over to watch another game, and while I'm here working she's ordering pizza online for us. She's awesome!*

And then I remembered the peonies.

And I thought: *Oh my god, I'm having one of those moments!*

Those spontaneous moments that we talked about. Those moments that "romantic" guys have and, more importantly, act on! I'm thinking of my love for her, I'm thinking of peonies, so there's only one thing to do: get my woman peonies! I shut down the computer. I raced out to the car. I headed right for the fancy florist on San Vicente that I went to on Valentine's Day. Closed on Sunday. This just made me more determined! I went to a florist on Montana. No peonies. Now it was starting to get late . . . The guys were coming over in a half hour and the Celtics were playing the Lakers in game one of the NBA finals. And what did I do? I went to another florist! Damn right that's what I did! And why did I take the chance of missing the tip-off? Because she my woman. (That's not a typo; I meant to say "she my woman" to show how deep and guttural and just plain feral I feel about her.) And here's another reason I wasn't giving up: In the pantheon of stupid things men say to women, "I was thinking about buying you flowers" is right up there. I didn't want to be *that* guy. And it's not like I hadn't been him before. In a lame effort to receive credit for a job well intentioned but not well done one says, "I was thinking about buying you flowers"—which is a cousin to "I didn't think you wanted me to take the trash out." Which is then only trumped in the world of stupidity by *"I didn't think you wanted an orgasm."*

Knowing all this I got myself quickly to another florist. And guess what? The florist had peonies! I went home and presented her with the peonies. Her heart soared! Our love went to the next level! And we fit in a quickie before the guys came over! NONE OF THAT HAPPENED.

What did happen was this: The florist had two peonies left. *Who knew fucking peonies were so popular?!* One peony was fully in bloom, the other was shut tight, scheduled for blooming on Tuesday or Wednesday. *Okay,* I thought, *I've still got two peonies*—granted, one of them is closed up, but still . . . it's something. And I was having my spontaneous moment. If there had been seventy peonies I would have got them for her. Price was no object for my love. But there were two. (Well, one and a half.) So do I wait for another day? Am I not then that guy who was *thinking* about buying her flowers? Okay, so it wasn't exactly how I pictured it, but still, I pulled the trigger and bought the flowers. It was my third florist and the way Kobe played against the Spurs, the game could have been over ten minutes after tip-off. So I bought the peonies, added a few other flowers, and got her a small vase. (She later said it was a "bud" vase but I felt that was derogatory.) So the flower lady made up the vase and I filled out the little card. And I wrote on it, "This is only the beginning." That's right. This was two peonies for now with several peonies to be named later. "This is only the beginning." But the two—okay, one and a half—peonies were to show that I actually had the "spontaneous thing" and acted on it.

I figured she'd be overjoyed. Okay, maybe not overjoyed, but at least *joyed.* I mean, it was like an appetizer for more romance to come. "This is only the beginning," I wrote with all its exquisite meanings for our future. It's only the beginning for peonies. It's only the beginning for *us.* When I presented the flowers she asked, why flowers? Why now? I told her to read the card, on which I had also written, "Because roses suit you so."

Unfortunately, it turns out that peonies aren't roses—although I maintain they're in the rose family. (They look like pinkish-type roses!) And the line "roses suit you so" is from some song from a musical I heard once. A romantic song! Okay, so I got the *type* of flower wrong on the card in an effort to be poetic and stole a Jerry Herman lyric; she should still appreciate them, right?

No. She didn't.

Of course in the moment, before the guys arrived, she smiled sweetly. And our eyes met, but I wasn't meeting bedroom eyes. I was meeting slightly confused, slightly-irritated-but-not-because-of-an-allergy eyes. But in the moment she seemed fine and pleased, if not bowled over. It wasn't until the next night that my solid romantic efforts came back to haunt me.

She started crying about the flowers.

Why didn't I get her more? Was I being cheap? Was I just lazy? One of the flowers in the "bud vase" wasn't even open . . . I reminded her of what I'd written on the card. She said, *"The part where you said they were roses?"* No! The other part, I reminded her, where I wrote "This is only the beginning." She didn't get that it meant there would be more flowers to come. But what was she supposed to think, given my spotty track record of flower giving? *"Last year you blew off peony season altogether!"*

Oh god.

(Okay, I didn't mean to blow it off, but by the time I finally made it to the florist last year those fake pink roses were out of season!)

So now she's distraught about the crappy little peonies. And I'm distraught that she's distraught about the crappy little peonies.

To review: Flowers, effort, expressing spontaneous love with something she likes.

The result: Tears. Complaints of not knowing her. And accusations of cheapness.

WHAT ABOUT THE EFFORT, WOMAN? WHAT ABOUT THE LOVE THAT WAS OBVIOUSLY COURSING THROUGH MY VEINS WHEN I BOUGHT THEM? WHAT ABOUT GOING TO THREE DIFFERENT PLACES!? I MEAN, JEESH, NOW YOU'RE UPSET WHEN I GET YOU FLOWERS? GOOD GOD, WHAT THE HELL DO WOMEN WANT?!

I couldn't believe that my grand gesture could have produced such unhappiness.

She then felt bad for feeling bad but couldn't take away her original bad feeling. There was confusion and dismay around our house for the next few days. I wanted to see her side of the story. I wanted to understand. But I couldn't quite grasp it. The one sure thing I'd always thought about our relationship was that if I walked in the door and unexpectedly presented her with peonies it would fill her with joy. It didn't. And I didn't know what to do. I felt like a failure. But I also felt that she was ungrateful. But mostly, I felt like I'd never understand her. Then a few days later she said something seemingly innocuous and it all started to fall into place . . .

SOFT AROUND THE RIM

"They're soft around the rim," she said.

"*What?!*" I look up from my part of the paper, confused.

"They're soft around the rim. *The Lakers.* That's what's going on with Gasol and Odom. Garnett and Perkins are stronger and tougher and boxing them out because these guys aren't as physical. The Lakers are soft around the rim."

At first I thought I must have died and gone to some kind of crazy sports heaven. But then I realized that I was still on earth and Jenny was reading from the L.A. *Times* sports page about the basketball game we'd watched the night before.

That's right. She was reading the sports page.

This is a women who, when the *New York Times* arrives, reaches first for the style page. She gets *Us, Elle,* and *Vogue,* and nary a gander has she ever taken at my *Sports Illustrated* or *ESPN the Magazine.* (I've actually never looked at *ESPN the Magazine,* it just came one day and won't stop coming.) So she has absolutely no prior knowledge of sports—or interest in them—and now she's telling me how the Lakers are perimeter shooters and how Phil Jackson's triangle offense might finally be letting them down. We then proceeded to engage in an almost barroom-like dissection of the game.

Jenny had watched the game the night before with me and, truth be told, scolded me when I turned it off. The Celtics (my team) were down by twenty-six points early and I was in agony. I figured she'd be thrilled that I abandoned this particular game. But that's not the Jenny I sometimes know. She accused me of being a fair-weather fan—to which I explained that I'm a realist and went on to other business. A few minutes later, she flipped the TV to the game and I barked at her, "Could you turn it off please?!" But she wanted to stick with it. Then my son came down and I had to explain to him that the Celtics, now twenty points behind in the third quarter, had no chance in hell. He said they were going to win, sat down next to Jenny, and we were back watching the game.

And it turned into the greatest comeback in basketball history.

And it was Jenny who turned the TV back on. And it was my son who insisted they were going to win—which I just chalked up to youthful innocence. He couldn't be right, could he? She couldn't be right in insisting that a true fan has to stick it out no matter what the score. Except they were both right. But what can possibly explain why Jenny is reading from the sports page and telling me that the Lakers are soft around the rim?

Jenny throws herself into whatever I'm interested in.

She gets excited about what I'm excited about—or at least tries hard to. She goes full bore. She doesn't hold back. She sat with me every Sunday during football season and well into the playoffs, and she was there for me during the crushing defeat of the Patriots in the Super Bowl. (She even got us a candy/nut dish in the shape of a Patriots helmet.) If there's a game that matters to me—and there are a lot lately—she's the first one to order pizza.

Which brings us back to peonies.

Yes, peonies.

And it's not that far a leap.

If a woman tells a man she likes peonies, then the man must find out every damn thing there is to know about peonies. He should find out where they're grown. Where they come from. What colors they come in. How they got their name. Where they have the best ones. What's the ideal time of day to get them. He should have his own peony guy on retainer. He should shower her with peonies every chance he gets. Lots of them. What he probably *shouldn't do* is get her one and a half peonies and write a cryptic card with a vague promise of more. And what he really shouldn't do is tell her that she's unknowable to him when she's actually told him everything he needs to know.

Men always think women want us to read their minds. And they do. Usually after they've told us everything we need to know fifty times leading up to the moment when we're supposed to magically "read their minds." Okay, yes, women are a difficult lot. For sure. They are like memory itself, made up of a perplexing and unreliable substance. They are a story that's ever changing depending on the teller. They are the most inconsistent species on the planet. One needs to know not only *her,* but the her she is *now.* Not the her she was when you first met her, or even, for that matter, the her she was *five minutes ago.*

If all this knowing stuff sounds tiring it's because it is! And ultimately it's every man's choice how much of the vast landscape of the female body and mind he's going to explore. But just like your third-grade teacher told you, "What you get out of something is directly proportional to what you put in."

But in those dark moments of frustration, fear, and even rage—when the distance to her heart and mind seems just too damn far—all the once open roads seem like dead ends. When you drive to her very center and all that is reflected back to you is an opaque nothingness, just when there seems to be no way in, perhaps try a different path.

Here's a tip: They're soft around the rim.

JENNY'S RESPONSE

HE LOVES ME? HE LOVES ME NOT? HOW DO I KNOW IF I DON'T HAVE FLOWERS TO TELL ME?!

When I read Howard's last chapter (which is my favorite) I found it incredibly touching and I was amazed at his progress not only as a boyfriend, but as a human being. As a woman I find myself perhaps at times too cynical about men learning new tricks (yes, I know the expression is old dogs, but close enough). Even six months earlier in our relationship the whole peony thing would have gone a different way—raised voices and tears, hurt feelings, and storming out of rooms (Howard may have even been upset too). There is a reason why hurricanes used to be named only after women, but this time the hurricane was downgraded to a tropical storm, or even a light shower with a rainbow. He took the time to understand what was going on and then he righted the wrong. The second bouquet of peonies he sent me was extraordinary. His achievement was worthy of a standing ovation. He deserved to take his bows. He brought hope to the nation.

After that, four months passed, and nothing.

It was as if he was Julius Caesar, who, having conquered Rome and gotten the salad named after him, just moved on. Trust me, there were definitely some times that I could have used some more flowers in the four long months that passed, but instead I waited. As I waited I wondered whether I was being a diva by wanting flowers on a regular basis, but I decided that it wasn't too much to ask for. And it's not like I just expected him to read my mind; I didn't. During the whole peony thing I definitely let him know that I would really be happy if I got flowers more often, and I just assumed after his peony triumph there would be a new era of flowers and romance.

But I was wrong.

I wondered if he thought he was off the hook because peony season lasts only a few months a year. When was he going to ask me about my second-favorite flower? What I realized is that he was coasting, like a kid on a bicycle going down a hill with his eyes closed, wheeeee . . .

To be fair I don't want to cast Howard as the bad guy when it comes to this, because this is not an issue of bad or good, or even right or wrong. As this has been an ongoing issue from the beginning of our relationship it has definitely crossed into the realm of stupid vs. crazy. But I know I'm accountable in the conflict and will readily admit to being crazy when it comes to flowers. I will step forward and admit that I have flower baggage. By this I do not mean I carry floral bags, or even carry flowers in actual bags, but that I have emotional baggage when it comes to flowers, specifically over all the flowers that I have yet to receive.

I suppose if I had to track down the origin of my flower angst it must have been from those flower days in high school when you could send carnations to your classmates for a dollar, white and pink ones to signify friendship, and red ones that meant love. All day long pep rally girls would appear in the doorways of classrooms, and all I could do was just sit there and try not to squirm. It took all my energy to pretend not to care, staring down at my desk unable to make eye contact for fear that my true feelings would be painfully clear. (The true feelings being that I was basically down on my knees praying to the gods that were in charge of high school to please just let my name be called.)

Don't worry, there is no need to brace yourself for the big sob story about how I never got one solitary carnation ever, or how I got one and it ended up being from my father. I definitely received a smattering of carnations on those days, but I was never the girl who received four or five every single period, until by the end of the day she had to have some of her less fortunate friends help her carry her great bounty around like a queen needing help with the train of her gown.

My high school boyfriend, Bryan Huddleston, may have inadvertently been a little to blame for my flower lust later in life. Bryan was the perfect high school boyfriend, very earnest and full of small-town Southern charm. He wrote me love notes, carried my books (this was the South; it was still done in the eighties), offered me his class ring to wear, and one year, on February 13, I received a dozen-plus-one red roses.

Whenever I got called to the principal's office over the intercom I was never too worried. Academically, I was a straight-A student, so as far as I was concerned, it meant either someone was dead or I got flowers. On that day I got flowers. The flowers were the classic long-stemmed red roses with lots of baby's breath (which I proceeded to pick out right there and throw away; even back then I was not a girl who liked filler). They were unwieldy, heavy, and housed in an ugly green vase, but I didn't care. There is no greater feeling than being a teenage girl walking through the halls of high school carrying a massive bouquet of flowers. Lunchtime in the cafeteria was never more magical than when you were sitting with your friends with a massive bouquet of red roses right next to you. It was like a beacon showing the world that here sits a girl who is very special and very loved.

Now, you are probably thinking what I was thinking: *February 13? Why would your boyfriend send you flowers one day before Valentine's Day?* Well in my delusional immature brain, I just assumed that this was "just the beginning" (hmmmm, perhaps Howard's words on the first peonies' card gave me a flashback to 'Nam). I thought that he was just warming up for the big Valentine's Day. When I saw him I threw myself into his arms with glee. How sweet that he wanted to single me out early; how great that he sent one more rose over the typical boring old dozen, and boy oh boy how great that tomorrow would bring something even more amazing.

I never say this cloying Southern expression, but it's deserved here with all sincerity as I look back on this day with twenty years of hindsight: Bless his heart. Because there had been an error at the flower store and they sent them on the wrong day. Being that his after-school job was bagging groceries at our local Kroger supermarket, Bryan had blown all of his cash on this particular arrangement, so on Valentine's Day there was nothing else coming. Being that he was seventeen and scared to death of what would happen when he told me, he said nothing.

So the next day when all the girls were being called to the front office to pick up their flowers or carrying their own large arrangements through the hallway, there I was, carrying nothing but my own foolish flower expectations. By the end of the day I was completely baffled and hurt, my previous day's flower joy already long gone. After school I met Bryan in our usual spot in the parking lot and when I saw him I burst into tears. He had no choice but to confess that the flowers from the previous day were an accident and he felt so bad that I found myself feeling even worse. I just kept asking him why he didn't tell me yesterday, which would have certainly spared me an entire day of waiting. He tried to cheer me up, saying that it was more special to receive flowers one day earlier as opposed to today when everyone had flowers.

Yes, everyone but me.

Howard stopped me here when I told this story. It's just too sad and too terrible for me to continue with. "Poor Bryan Huddleston," he says.

"Poor Bryan Huddleston? What about me?!"

As a guy, Howard only had sympathy for Bryan. And he especially felt his pain as the topic of flowers has been an ongoing one in our two-year relationship. Right from the get-go when Howard and I started dating I gave him a heads-up. I let him know I was high maintenance, which I explained was much better than those girls who said they were low maintenance and didn't know they were high maintenance. By "high maintenance" I didn't mean private jets and a pied-à-terre in Paris, but that I'm a girl who knows what she likes and I just happen to like flowers and thoughtful presents. I also assured him that I am very laid-back when it comes to a lot of other areas where other women get uptight (e.g., I'm not a nagger and I'm never going to make him go clean the garage), so it would all balance out.

He seemed to be listening when I made my pronouncement, yet somehow he didn't seem to hear what I was actually saying. Now looking back I should have drawn up a relationship contract to let him know that flowers were just a standard part of my deal when it comes to being a girlfriend:

Heretofore, Jenny Lee, hereby known as GIRLFRIEND, will require flowers on a regular basis over and above the standard flower times like Valentine's Day, anniversary, birthday, promotions, hospital stays, etc. GIRLFRIEND will expect a regular stream of bouquets to just show that you love her, adore her,

couldn't live without her, are thinking of her, are wondering what
she's thinking about, are sorry that she's having a bad day, and
to just let her know that she of all people in the whole wide world
deserves to have flowers on her desk.

a) Let it also be known that GIRLFRIEND is not expecting
any old flowers. She expects BOYFRIEND to make proper in-
quiries about which particular flowers she finds most desirable.

I am obviously joking about such a contract, but Howard
tells me that he wishes I gave him one because it certainly
would have made his life easier. For a moment I think about
explaining to him that perhaps it might take away some of the
romance element if I have to do the work to make his life easier
when it comes to getting me flowers, but I don't say this. A little
surprise wouldn't be so bad, would it?

He points out that a woman who has such high expectations when it comes to flowers doesn't seem like she's in want
of a surprise. Because if that were so I would have been more
excited about the Flowers of the Month Club he just purchased
for me, which ensures twelve months of surprises.

When we were on the topic of flowers and how I want more
from him, I told him that the one thing I remember from the
fifteen-year-old movie *The Age of Innocence* is that Daniel Day-
Lewis's character had a standing order at the florist to provide
his betrothed, Winona Ryder, with her favorite flowers every
week. Her dressing table would never be barren of violets.
When I told Howard this he reminded me that things didn't
work out all too well for them in the end. And I said that I
doubted their tragic outcome was due to the flowers, and for
all we know it could have ended a lot worse.

So when I received the e-mail announcement that I had just been signed up for the Flowers of the Month Club, Howard had signed the e-mail card as Daniel Day Morris. Cute and funny definitely, but not to me at that very moment. There are many things that Howard can joke his way out of, because he is that funny of a guy. But to me this wasn't a laughing matter, and when I got the form e-mail announcing my gift I wasn't amused. We were at a standstill; he didn't understand what I wanted. And I didn't understand why he couldn't give it to me anyway.

When I've asked men (Howard included, as well as other male friends and ex-boyfriends) why they don't give the women they love flowers more often, I get a variety of responses: *I don't need to give flowers to show my love. I mean to, but I always forget. I'll do it next week. It always slips my mind. I guess I understand the appeal but I think they are a waste of money. I just never think about it.* And my favorite one of all time, *Why can't you just believe that I want to give you flowers all the time?*

No offense intended, but to me those are the lamest excuses I have ever heard. I mean, do they hear themselves? It's not like these guys are living in their parents' basements and don't have steady jobs. No, these guys are all top members of their fields, successful, driven, smart, yet somehow they just couldn't get it together to take care of this one thing. I mean, getting a girl flowers is hardly rocket science, right?

Whenever I see no end to me beating my forehead against the wall I try to look for a comparison that might help me understand Howard better, some sort of bridge in between how men and women think. So here's what I'm thinking: *Women who want flowers are similar to guys who want blow jobs.* (Now,

I'm not trying to be overtly sexual or provocative by saying this, so for the squeamish or shy, as I prove my thesis statement, I will replace the words "blow job" with "pizza." So when I say men love pizza, I don't want you to get confused and think, *Yes, that's true, men do love pizza.* I'll even italicize *"pizza"* to help remind you.)

Men love *pizza*. Most men don't feel they get as much *pizza* as they would like. Men would like to have *pizza* every day. I'm pretty sure if men got *pizza* every day there would be fewer wars and you could look out your window and see grown men skipping down the street and singing. As we women know, men rarely get *pizza* every day. In the beginning of a relationship men may get *pizza* a lot, and may even get *pizza* a few days in a row or even twice a day if they are lucky, but in general, I'm willing to climb out on a limb and wave to you from above and say that men don't get *pizza* as often as they would like. Men in relationships want more *pizza*.

Now, it would be wrong for you to take this analogy too literally, because I'm not saying it's an exact comparison. All I'm trying to explain is that women love flowers—probably not as much as men love *pizza*, but in a similarly wistful way. Now, there are men who love giving women flowers; c'mon, we've all heard the stories about such mythical beasts (the friend of a friend who is dating the centaur, etc.). And there are the men who dutifully give flowers at every major holiday (this being akin to the birthday *pizza* that men usually get!). And there are the men who, for whatever reason, just feel ambivalent about giving flowers to women and therefore don't do it often. Okay, do you see the similarities? And again, I'm not trying to be literal or sensational, or change the world here, this is just me wanting to share my own personal theory on flowers and *pizza*. (And I'm not really talking about flowers and *pizza* in the first six months of a relationship, because the first six months to a year everyone is on the ball and there is statistically speaking lots more flowers and *pizza*.)

When you really think about it, flowers and *pizza* are not things that can be called needs. Not like food, water, shelter, love, companionship, and cake. (Just joking about the cake, sort of.) Flowers and *pizza* do not make the world go 'round. No one will die without them. No one will fight to the death for them (well, no woman will). They are kind of like the cherry on the top. Or the sprinkles. Awesome to have, but you can still live a fine life without them. But why should you when you don't have to? So of course you want them. And shouldn't the person who loves you want you to have them? Flowers (and *pizza*) just make you feel good. And the good feelings last a while. Yay, I got flowers. Yay, I love flowers. Yay, I got flowers yesterday. Yay, I got *pizza*. Yay, I love *pizza*! Yay, I got *pizza* yesterday!

It's just that it's a struggle for me to understand why men don't give flowers more often. They are not hard to find. They don't have to be too expensive. They can't claim ignorance because it's totally obvious that this is something that's been going on through the ages. That's why it lasts, because it works. Sure, there might have been that one guy who gave his woman a shovel and a wheelbarrow and was like, "Hey, I was thinking since you like flowers so much that maybe you should grow them yourself." But I'm pretty sure that man is now buried at the bottom of the very flower bed he suggested.

Perhaps to better understand this mystery, I have to take a

hard and long look at my own personal attitude toward *pizza*. Howard loves *pizza*, and these days I'm pretty sure that he feels he doesn't get *pizza* enough. Truth be told, Howard used to get *pizza* all the time. But it has slowed down, considerably. (Though let the record show it's not like he ONLY gets *pizza* on special occasions like his birthday; sometimes he still gets surprised with a private *pizza* party here and there. I'm no fool; I don't want him to get desperate for *pizza* and start to feel the need to go out and buy *pizza* for himself at some random *pizza* parlor. No, that would be very bad.) So I guess I can now say that I have realized that perhaps I too am guilty of not indulging my man with enough *pizza*.

Okay, it's settled. I will stop complaining and just accept that men honestly forget to give flowers and that we shouldn't take their lack of flower giving quite so seriously. I will try, I promise. And as for all you men out there feeling deprived of *pizza*, just know that I get it and maybe this will make you feel better. "Oh, baby, why can't you just believe that we want to give you *pizza* all the time?"

8

GRATING EXPECTATIONS

STILL STUPID AFTER ALL THESE YEARS

I don't know what you loved in me /
Maybe the picture of somebody you were
hoping I might be.

—JACKSON BROWNE

It's probably clear from everything you've read so far that when it comes to women I'm pretty much a complete imbecile.

But it's worse than that.

Because I'm one of those guys who women *assume know better*.

And guys like us *do* have it worse. We're doomed to always let women down because they had such high hopes for us. I come across as sensitive and intelligent, wear glasses, and have had years of therapy. (I like talking about my feelings. I like it so much a former therapist once pleaded with me, "You know, you don't have to tell me *everything*.") So when a guy well-versed in the ways of emotions turns out to be an insensitive dolt, women find it all the more tragic. I've often lamented my fate and wished I could just be your average simple idiot. If this describes you, consider yourself blessed. (And if you're *really* a simple idiot perhaps you should get this book on tape.)

As for me, I'm forever doomed to crush the spirits of hopeful women. After hearing about another of my misadventures in the land of the fairer sex, my friend Susanne looked at me with the saddest expression I've ever seen. "It's so depressing," she said. "What?" I asked. *"That a guy like you isn't even a guy like you."*

That's me. A guy like me who isn't a guy like me.

But if a guy like me isn't a guy like me, when is a guy like me *actually a guy like me*? Who's a real guy like me? The guy I'm supposed to be. The guy I'm often *assumed* to be. The guy women believe actually knows a thing or two about them.

Who is *that* guy?

He doesn't exist.

Okay, wait! Before women throw this book across the room in utter disgust and hopelessness, let's talk about this! He does exist—*in moments*. We can all be the better part of ourselves for a moment or two. Maybe even for an hour. But at some point every guy, no matter how enlightened he is, reverts to being himself—which is to say that he becomes what he always was: a guy.

This seems to distress women to no end. Apparently, they were expecting someone else. "I forget sometimes that you're a guy," Jenny tells me often. "And then it hits me: you are." Uh, thanks. This is said, it should be noted, as if that weren't an extremely odd statement, and always in a tone that bespeaks her disappointment with this current state of affairs. She seems to have trouble reconciling the me she thought I was and the me who I *am*. And it's this very disparity between who we are and who they expected us to be that drives women freaking bananas. Women's expectations of the men they love have a way of running rampant and wreaking havoc on their brains.

And yet, they have the audacity to call it hope.

But what makes it really crazy is *it's not like they didn't know who we are*. But still, they keep expecting us to be someone else.

At first, Jenny's discovery of my inherent "guyness," despite her initial belief that I was some kind of sissy man, I suppose, wasn't exactly a problem for her. It just kind of threw her for a loop. I heard her on the phone one day talking to a friend. "Howard gets *Sports Illustrated*. Weird, huh? Does Chris get *Sports Illustrated*? . . . I didn't think so. Wow. I just never saw myself as one of those girls who is with a guy who gets *Sports Illustrated*."

I never saw myself having a Christmas tree, but I had one this year!

So what? Things change. I got over it. No expectations from this guy. First marriages are for expectations. Now I am a wiser and happier man. Sometimes when Jenny and I, who both have a first marriage behind us, act in a way that's unbecoming to our relationship, we each tell the other, "That's sooo first marriage." For instance, blaming your partner for your entire life is "sooo first marriage."

Expectations are also "sooo first marriage."

Here's the thing women don't realize: *All guys* get Sports Illustrated—at least metaphorically if not in the mail. (Even the sainted Chris!)

Expectations will kill you every time.

Jenny still can't get over a novel I wrote in my early thirties that is by turns brimming with youthful insight, sweetness and sensitivity, and chock-full of immature notions, broad juvenile humor, and pornographic sex. (With all this, it should be a better read . . .) It's the juxtaposition of these qualities—which obviously still reside in me—she can't seem to reconcile. It strikes a dissonant chord in how she perceives me. Something about my young man's novel still troubles her even after knowing me for two years. Something about it, *about me,* just doesn't make sense to her.

DANGER, WILL ROBINSON! DOES NOT COMPUTE!

It's a sex scene that she finds most disturbing. She's mentioned to me, repeatedly, how struck she was, how taken aback, how *surprised*—and not in a good way—she was when she read it. Now, it's not that Jenny Lee is an anti-sex-scene prude. She just finds *the way in which I wrote about sex* wanting. There's one passage that she always brings up—as if she's still trying to process how "her Howard" could have written it. It was clearly a definitive moment in her initial assessment of me, and one that gives her pause even today.

Here's the passage from my novel:

"As I sat down in the passenger seat I caught a glimpse of her delicately freckled left breast peeking out through the top of her V-neck. I had a powerful urge to hurdle over the stick shift and suckle that breast until the freckles came off in my mouth. I made sure my seat belt was fastened tight."

Her one-word review: "Ewww."

Okay, so it's not Philip Roth. But I'm not even sure why it's this particular passage that's burned a permanent, if unwanted, place in her brain—because I wrote much worse! Not to mention the interrupted masturbating scene (inspired no doubt by the master himself), or the scene where the woman's breasts did "a beautiful bobbing dance" as I "felt the full force of her body grinding against me." While "all the blood in my body rushed so completely to my penis I feared I might faint." There's also a quite a bit of "exploding inside her" after being "tenderly guided into her warm mouth."

I used the word "tender"! What's she complaining about?!

Okay, so it's more "Penthouse Forum" than D. H. Lawrence. (But of course, "Penthouse Forum" *was* a much bigger influence on me.) And while I might concur with her "Ewww" in regards to the quality of my writing, the male attitude about sex isn't far off. I mean, immature in its execution, yes, *but it is how guys see sex:* To us, it's a visceral, horny, boob-jiggling, "Penthouse Forum"–y kind of thing.

And women know this.

But somehow this wasn't what they were expecting.

What were they expecting? And who told them they should expect it? Do they really think that even the great McDreamy— second only to Chris in my house—speaks of sex with Meredith in a discreet English-accented whisper? "Her skin is sweet alabaster, dear George, and as soft as rose petals . . ."

Ewww.

Did they expect they could change us? In many cases, yes. (That's not just a subject for another chapter. That's a whole book.) Or did they just expect that we would mature to the point that we'd eventually be unrecognizable to ourselves? Was that the hope? Or perhaps the goal?

Even a guy like me isn't a guy like me.

Expectations will get you every time.

When women get to know us their expectations are inevitably lowered—and the craziness is somewhat lessened. But they never quite give up the expectation ghost or get over the initial shock of who we really are, despite their best efforts and hopes to the contrary. And this drives them insane—and in some cases to drink. But expectations also have a deleterious effect on men as well. *We snap under the weight of them.* We can't ever seem to fulfill women's expectations so we go the other way. We take an expectation and do the exact opposite—just for spite!

This never turns out well.

CRAZY EXPECTATIONS/STUPID RESPONSES

Just this morning, Jenny and I had a classic crazy expectation/ stupid response situation in our house. (Perhaps *the* classic crazy expectation/stupid response.) I went to kiss her good-bye on my way out of the shower and she pulled her head away. Kiss resisting is never good. "What's wrong?" I asked. "You didn't notice my hair," she answered, clearly hurt, and then brusquely turned away from me and walked down the stairs. I immediately yelled after her that it looked fabulous. From downstairs, she yelled up that I didn't even have my glasses on—making my assessment of her hair somewhat suspect. (Without my glasses, she might not have even *had* hair. I wouldn't know.)

But why do women expect we'll notice their hair? We never do.

Except when they change it radically. And then they're never happy with the way in which we notice it. "What the hell happened to your hair?" may not be subtle, but what were they expecting? And yet, the expectation persists—after trillions of new hairdos all over the world have gone unnoticed by men for generations.

Stupidly, I decided to fight the charges against me—talk about "sooo first marriage." I yelled down, "Jesus, Jenny, when you came home last night I was already in bed! I didn't even have my glasses on! And it was dark!" She then came to the foot of the stairs and looked up at me with her "You're such an idiot" expression. (I didn't need my glasses to see this.) *"We had dinner together last night,"* she said. Which I'm pretty sure would have been "We had dinner together last night, you imbecile" had my eight-year-old son not been in the near vicinity. After dinner tonight when I told her that *all* guys don't notice women's haircuts, she told me that *her ex-husband* always noticed.

That's sooo first-major-relationship-after-you're-divorced.

She has a crazy expectation and I react even more stupidly than normal.

It's expectations, my friends, once again doing their devil magic!

THE GIFT OF THE MORON

The expectations surrounding giving gifts in relationships are perfect opportunities for the crazy expectation/stupid response. Gift giving in any relationship is an art, and certainly most women are better at it, though I have received my share of gifts I wished had just remained as a picture in a catalog. Gift expectations work both ways with women: First there's the gift you give *her,* which comes with the expectation that it will somehow show that you know her and that you put thought and effort into it. Fair enough. But then there's also the expec-

tation a woman has when she gives *you* a gift: the expectation
that you'll see the gift exactly as she sees it—which is how she
sees you and by extension how *you should see you*. And then of
course you'll thank her profusely for it.

For my thirtieth birthday, my ex-wife gave me ten sessions
with a trainer. "Happy birthday, fatty!" the gift seemed to be
saying. "Now get in shape, tubbo!" was clearly the expectation
accompanying that gem of a present. (And this was years before
"the Stick" signaled the end of our union was near.) When I reacted with less than utter glee on my face, she got upset. Then
I had to console *her* about my reaction to *my* gift and assure
her that, yes, I was a fatty, and thank god she got me a trainer,
which I could never have had the courage to get for myself.

A particularly ill-fitting birthday gift I once received was
from a newish girlfriend who belonged to a country club—an
extremely Waspy country club, it should be noted. I've never
been a country club guy. I'm not a joiner, as Groucho Marx said.
And certainly not at this beach club—which in its infamous
history did not allow Jews or blacks in for decades. So imagine
my surprise when she handed me "an outfit I could wear to the
beach club on Sunday afternoons!" It was an extremely preppy
shirt (if it didn't have an alligator on it, it should have) and
jaunty white pants.

White pants.

I've never really been a white pants kind of guy. And I knew
that the clothes came with an expectation that I would be the
kind of country-club-going fellow-well-met who would accom-
pany her and her children there every Sunday for the rest of my
life. I totally cracked under the "white pants" expectation. But
instead of gently trying to right her wrong impression of me,

by perhaps calmly discussing things with her at an appropriate moment, I decided one night to make sure she knew who I was and who I wasn't.

After sex. *Like right after.*

If anyone can dim the shimmering light of an afterglow, it's me. Let's just say that during the postcoital cuddle no one wants to hear about the history of anti-Semitism in America. I also mentioned that night—with the subtlety of a falling anvil—that I wasn't sure I could deal with her little children. *Right after sex.*

I cracked under the expectations, what can I tell you?!

Not surprisingly, she dumped me the next day. Surprisingly, we've remained friends to this day. Not surprisingly, I've never worn those white pants.[1]

But no matter how inured I was to getting gifts that come with expectations (the stick, the trainer, the white pants), nothing could have prepared me for what Jenny Lee said to me several days before our second anniversary of being together. Since I'd been forbidden from entering her loft/studio in our house for weeks, I knew she was working on something for me, and since she had recently been taking art classes, I assumed it was some kind of painting—which I knew I would love, because she's a wonderful painter with a wicked sense of humor in her work. What I didn't expect was what she told me one morning: *"It's the most meaningful gift I've ever given anyone."*

HOW AM I SUPPOSED TO HANDLE THE EXPECTATIONS THAT COME WITH THAT SENTENCE?!

---

[1] Jenny has expressed her concern to me that in this book she's coming off as "too crazy." I try to reassure her that she's coming off "just the right amount of crazy." However, now I'm concerned that with the revelation of my postcoital faux pas, I'm going to be forever remembered as the idiot who couldn't shut up after he came.

Again, two issues: How do I match the most meaningful gift *ever*? I can't just pick her up a few tchotchkes at the "Meaningful Store." (By the way, not a bad idea for a business; it could be very convenient for guys buying gifts.) And then there's the question of *my reaction* to receiving the most meaningful gift ever. I better love it! And be effusive in my love for it. I better muster up a tear or two, or even weep uncontrollably from being so moved, or I'll risk letting her down, or worse, pissing her off.

So naturally, my first instinct was to go the other way.

Way the other way.

Gift certificate to Sizzler.

"Hey, so, uh . . . just know that you mean a lot more to me than this gift would suggest." Okay, that's beyond-the-pale stupid. But I understand the impulse. Hell, I've *acted on* that impulse before. I've made the choice to do the stupid/jerky thing in an attempt to subvert expectations and show women that I'm a rebel who goes his own way. But now my own way was probably where I'd be going.

But I also knew that what made Jenny's gift so meaningful was that she was *making it* for me and spending an incredible amount of time on it. *So I'll build her a cabin!* I thought. Except that I can't build and where would we put a cabin anyway? Second thought: *I'll make her something artistic and meaningful out of papier-mâché!* Oh man, that's just creepy. And I'll just end up eating the paste . . .

DAMN YOU, EXPECTATIONS! I HAVE NO CHOICE BUT TO ACT STUPIDLY!

Expectations make every day Valentine's Day—a day with expectations so rampant it's battered even the most solid of couples. Expectations killed New Year's Eve! When you're a kid you watch the stupid ball drop and you're off to bed. But no one in the history of adult relationships has ever had a good New Year's Eve because of the expectations placed on that night by women!

Okay, that's not always true.

Our first New Year's Eve was phenomenal. (As I talked about in chapter 4.) But it was the *one and only* great New Year's Eve of my life. And it never would have happened had we had big expectations. We both had been burned too many times by overpriced prix fixe menus and drunken revelers puking on our shoes to expect that this night would be different. But it turned out to be romantic and sexy and the food was great and the restaurant had a stunning view of downtown Los Angeles. But you know what happens when you have a great New Year's Eve? It creates even bigger expectations for the next year! Predictably, the next year sucked. We were back in prix fixe hell, only able to get a too-early reservation, and yet early enough to be surrounded by drunken idiots puking on our shoes. But even worse, the great steakhouse I had promised her was *serving fish that night.* And they wouldn't let us get the sweet potato fries, or the macaroni and cheese, or any of the "sides" that make the place *the place*. (The mac and cheese makes you want to change your religion or start a new one.)

Prix fixe menus were obviously invented by guy chefs chafing under the expectations of Valentine's Day and New Year's Eve. Why else would the food always disappoint on all those romantic holiday nights? The chef knows chicks are coming to his restaurant with hopes and dreams of unparalleled romance, so he freaks out and says to himself, "I know! I'll cook something I suck at!" Stupid, yes. Incomprehensible, no.

The culprit here, as always, is the E word.

If we could just put an end to expectations, I firmly believe we could once and for all eliminate misery in between men and women. And if I am elected president of relationships, I will *outlaw* expectations. I will put in our party's platform that if one must expect anything, then expect the worst and be pleasantly surprised! But let's remove this burden of hopes and dreams for our boyfriends once and for all. In fact, don't expect anything from anybody—especially the people you love.

But here's what the woman running against me for president of relationships would say in her convention speech: *"Is our opponent suggesting we just abandon all standards of behavior? That we should just expect nothing of a man? Is that what it's come to? That we shouldn't even hope now? We should just give and give and expect nothing in return? Aren't expectations part of what a relationship is? The expectation that the other person will be there for you in ways that are deeply meaningful for you? Doesn't every human being have the right to expect to be taken care of, to be loved, to be supported emotionally? Aren't expectations the very essence of a relationship? If we have no expectations of one another, then are we really anything to each other at all?"*

Okay, well . . . uh, yeah, I sorta get that . . .

But why does it mean I have to wear white pants on New Year's Eve while perusing an overpriced prix fixe menu that I can't eat anything off of anyway because of my trainer, who's going to make me go on a hike with a stupid walking stick?!

Because there are expectations and there are expectations.

And it behooves one to know the difference.

There are expectations that expect you to be a whole different person, and then there are expectations that you'll be the best person you are. The person the other person fell in love with. Stupid isn't that stupid to act stupid if someone wants to change stupid's whole personality. But for stupid to act stupid when someone truly loves him for who he is is unforgivably stupid. And crazy may be crazy to expect a man to not be a man, or even, frankly, to notice her hair, but there's nothing crazy about expecting to be loved the way one needs to be loved.

To put it simply: I better get her a good fucking gift.

THE MOST MEANINGFUL GIFT EVER

It's a painting. But it's not. It's a collage. But it's not. It's decoupage. But it's not. It's a series of photographs. But it's not. It's an antique. But it's not. But it is a work of art. And it took my breath away.

In those hours up in her loft, Jenny took an old scratchy photo strip of us that we'd taken in a photo booth and transformed it into something magical. The poses on the strip are funny, hammy, goofy, sexy (her, not me), and surprisingly sincere. She enlarged some of the photos, minimized others, mixed them up, shellacked some, painted over others, wrote the word "love" in places in and around them, played with colors, tone, surfaces, textures, brought out the scratches in some for effect, and blotted out the scratches in others for equal but different effect. It's really only four different poses of us but it looks like a thousand. And after all the coats of shellac, visits to Kinko's, painting, repainting, gluing, placing, and replacing the pictures in all their various sizes, she captured the essence of us. She captured our love.[2]

I gave her a silver charm bracelet.

Okay, okay, I thought it might be cheesy, too. But cheesy with meaning always trumps cheesy. Here are the charms I chose to put on the bracelet:

- A heart that says "Happy Anniversary"—Because it commemorated the occasion and let me inscribe the date we met on the back.
- A book—Because she's a writer and a voracious reader of them.
- A laptop computer—Because it's the instrument she uses to write her books.
- A football helmet—Because she's embraced my passion for the game as if it's her own. (Even if she is a Dallas Cowboys fan.)
- An easel with different paints—Because it's the thing she uses to paint pictures that make my son and me laugh and shake our heads in amazement and delight.
- A Newfoundland dog—Because we have Doozy, a Newfie that she loves even more than me.
- A stop sign that says "I'll never STOP loving you"—Because we know how important signs are to her. And I won't.

---

[2] In a bit of delicious irony, the pictures we took in the photo booth that so clearly captured our crazy/stupid love for each other, that Jenny used as the basis of her painting, were taken in a photo booth at Jonathan Silverman's wedding party! Yes, he had a photo booth there. Okay, maybe it's not delicious. But it is irony, considering the night we were about to have . . .

She cried when I gave it to her. In the good way.

Expectations fulfilled on both sides. Who knew?

Later that night, we went out to dinner at a fun restaurant on the pier in Santa Monica, with a plan to then ride the famous Ferris wheel—which she's wanted to do for some time. Our dinner was excellent—no prix fixe for anniversaries, thank god—and we enjoyed a stunning view of the pier. I was well into my second raspberry mojito (their specialty) and feeling oh-so-fine when I noticed something a bit distracted in her look. She pointed to the Ferris wheel, which was lit up beautifully with lights beaming off of it in all different colors and patterns. "It's not running," she said. I then saw that although it was lit up, the wheel itself was not rotating. I checked my watch. It was already well past eight.

"Maybe they close it early on weeknights," I said, before assuring her that we would go another night.

She nodded and smiled her "making the best of it" smile.

"What?" I said.

"Nothing," she lied.

"What?!"

"I'm trying not to see it as a sign."[3]

---

[3] See chapter 7.

JENNY'S RESPONSE

WHAT TO EXPECT WHEN YOU'RE EXPECTING PIZZA

One of the nicest parts about having a boyfriend or a husband is that you get to feel like you are a part of a team. You can't be a couple on your own, you can't be "we" when it's just you, and you certainly can't expect to ever win a three-legged race all by yourself. As much as it's great to have someone to share your happiest times with, there is also a comfort to knowing that you automatically have someone on your side when you face challenges as well.

Howard is great when I wake up from a bad dream, never gets mad when I forget my keys when I walk the dog, and as he is prone to getting up a lot in the middle of the night, he never seems to mind if I ask him for water or Advil or a hug during his nocturnal wanderings. Howard is a guy who is dependable a hundred and one percent. (Though if we were shipwrecked and ended up on a desert island I think that I would survive longer alone, as Howard is definitely the guy who would use our last remaining flare to look for his glasses that he lost in the sand. But when it comes to living on a desert island, to me quality of time is far more important than quantity of time.)

Navigating modern-day life is tough; there are lots of de- cisions, lots of different schedules, and as a couple you can either work together or against each other. In general, Howard and I are a well-oiled machine of awesome coupleness. We are very compatible in our daily lives: We both make punctuality a priority; we both would rather do takeout than deal with cooking and dishes; and our most famous, albeit most sickening, couple-y thing we say (and for the record he said it first) is that we make each other laugh so often it's like a slumber party every night. My biggest complaint about some of Howard's chapters is that he is always focusing on the negative aspects of our relationship, so you can imagine my surprise when I read in his chapter that he's having trouble dealing with my expectations. I don't think I've ever complained one time of him not meeting my expectations (besides the flowers), because most of the time he fulfills them, and on a few occasions he's even surpassed them.

The other night I finished my art class and I was thinking I'd pick up dinner when I saw that Howard had texted me that he had already ordered our dinner and it was ready to be picked up. I smiled because he had impeccable timing, which greatly impressed me. But I had the thought, like a soap bubble floating up from the kitchen sink, *I wonder what kind of pizza Howard ordered for me?* I thought this because number one, I usually do all the ordering, and number two, I am quite particular about my pizza, whereas Dustin and Howard are pretty simple in their pizza tastes.

I called him from the car and said I was on my way to pick up dinner. "So what kind of pizza did you get me?" Howard, smiling—I can always tell by his voice—said, "Half-vegetable and half-plain just in case you don't like the vegetable." He was proud of himself that he had a backup plan just in case. This again shows his thoughtfulness, because he knows I'm a girl who loves a good contingency plan. *But why would we need a contingency plan when it came to pizza?*

When I got home with the food the table had been set, and again, I was struck by how damn compatible we were. Setting the table and making my bed were two things that were mandatory my entire adolescent life, which is why I no longer do either. But I found a guy who does the two things that I don't like to! I mean, compatible city, right?

So as Dustin and Howard were digging into their large pizza (half extra sauce and light cheese for Howard, and half regular sauce and cheese for Dustin) I was staring at the smaller pizza box that was open before me.

He gets a total pass on the sliced tomatoes that were on top. I totally know that it's weird that I don't like sliced tomatoes. I don't like them on sandwiches, I don't like them on hamburgers, and I don't like them on pizza. But I don't mind them diced up in salsa or on most Mexican food. I also really like tomato sauce. So obviously, my relationship with tomatoes is complicated.

But what really startled me was the presence of olives.

I. Do. Not. Like. Olives.

There is no confusion to be had about this one. I don't like them. I don't like them. I don't like them. They are one of those things that if they were in a dish, near a dish, or even the only food left on earth, I would not eat it. I would not have let them share my rescue raft if we had been on the *Titanic* together. I would not stop to help an olive change its flat tire on the side of the road, and if that seems really cold-hearted of me, just know, I wouldn't expect the olive to stop for me. Me and olives do not get along.

I took a deep breath, and then I let the whole thing go and just started picking them off the pizza without a word. There used to be a time when having my boyfriend get me a pizza with olives would have put me over the edge. *How does he not know me? Was it a passive-aggressive mistake? Was it just plain aggressive-aggressive?* Pizza, these days, is a very big deal in our house (we are all trying to eat better so it's not often we indulge), and in fact the last time we got pizza the whole experience was ruined for me because there was olive pesto on my mushroom pizza when I specifically asked for them not to use it. On that occasion I didn't completely flip out (it was I who ordered the pizza), but there was a lot of old-school Greek-tragedy lamenting happening in our house over the pizza parlor's grave error. I was channeling Clytemnestra big-time with all my hand waving and ruing. *"From Ida's top Hephaestus, lord of fire / Sent forth my call to the pizza parlor. Hear they not I say no olives / no olives, not one, I repeated!"* But I now get that Howard was not listening to my theatrics, because otherwise there is no way he couldn't have known that I am the archenemy of olives after all the racket I made.

But no matter, because I was letting it go.

I know one requirement of letting something go is to actually *let it go,* which means not bringing it up later. So I didn't bring up the olives specifically, but what I did do was subtly bring up the whole notion of whether Howard knew me from Eve.

"Howard?"

"Yeah?"

"Do you remember that old game show *The Newlywed Game*?"

"In the butt, Bob!"

"Excuse me?"

Howard started laughing and explained that there is an urban legend that once on the show, the host Bob asked a contestant where was the strangest place she ever made whoopee and she replied, "In the butt, Bob."

Okay, I must have missed that one. And sure, it wasn't really how I expected this conversation to begin, but I continued anyway.

"How do you think we would do on *The Newlywed Game*?"

Howard's whole posture stiffened and reminded me of that childhood game Frozen Statues, where everyone had to twirl around and around as fast as they could until someone yelled out, "Frozen statues!" At which time you had to freeze in whatever pose you were in like a, well, a frozen statue. (The winner was the one who was the funniest frozen statue.) Howard looked frozen exactly like that, eyes big, shoulders raised high, and it was a toss-up on whether he was even breathing.

"Relax, this is not a conversation about marriage."

He let out all the breath he was holding and wiped his brow. I made no notice and continued. "I'm just wondering how you think we'd do if we were contestants on the show."

Howard, who likes to tell me that he knows me better than anyone else on the planet, cut right through my bullshit.

"Is this about the olives?"

I shrugged and tried to give him my best innocent look. No way I was gonna say the word "olives" in this conversation, because I had let that whole thing go! (Though I did wonder if I could now talk about them since he brought them up.)

I played it safe. "No, this is not about . . . *Those things.*"

He scrutinized me very intensely but I didn't look away. He told me again that he knows me better than anyone else. I didn't say anything back. But in my head I thought of all the people who know me who also know I don't like olives on my pizza. It's not a small number. I stuck to my toy guns and did not say anything. *This is not about the olives.*

The next morning Howard called me as soon as he got to his office.

"What's this e-mail?"

"What e-mail?"

"This e-mail I got from Heather with the subject line 'The Newlywed/Live Together Game.'"

"Ohhhh, *that* e-mail. This morning Heather is not your assistant, she's our awesome game show host. I just thought that maybe it'd be fun if we play. All the questions she picked were actual questions from the original game."

He sighed, and I knew he was wondering whether this was really the best use of his assistant's time that day, but he didn't say that. Instead he asked, "Is this about the olives?"

"No." I stood firm. "I just thought it might be fun."

"C'mon, Jenny, I hate taking tests and you have to know that I know you the right way—the important way—and the olives don't mean anything! Maybe I don't know exactly how you take your pizza, but I know what's in your heart."

If you knew what was in my heart then you would know there are no olives there.

"Please. It'll be fun."

"I hate this stuff, and I test poorly."

"It's not a test. It's a game show! Now, c'mon, Mama needs a new washer-dryer!"

"What?"

"I'm just trying to act like a proper contestant. Who knows? Maybe we'll win the grand prize."

Howard doesn't say anything, but it's obvious he thinks he's already lost having to put up with a nut job like me.

Heather did the whole thing by e-mail. Two rounds, ten questions each. In the first round, Howard had to answer questions about me that he thought I would give the same answers to. In the next round he had to answer questions about himself. He had to name my favorite comfort food, how many pairs of shoes I would say that I had, and my dream vacation. I had to list his shoe size, what he would be if he could change professions, his dream car, and where he'd go if someone gave him a week's vacation anywhere on the planet.

I answered seven out of the ten questions correctly. Howard, one and a half out of ten.[4]

Now even though I officially got three wrong, I really only missed one question. While Heather was scoring my answers, I predicted two of the answers that Howard would give to questions about me that were actually wrong, but I knew he would choose them. So unofficially, I did get nine out of ten questions right, and I felt pretty satisfied.

There was a time when I would have found great satisfaction in trying this case, *The State of the Relationship vs. Howard J. Morris,* where I would prove that he was wrong and that the fact that he didn't know the answer to such questions about me did *indeed* mean that he didn't love me as much as he thought

---

[4] Heather was nice and gave him half a point because on one question where I was asked what habit would I break of Howard's if I could, I had replied, "None. Howard's an original, I'll take all his habits good and bad." And Howard had answered, "Jenny thinks I'm perfect." He meant it as a joke, but it was still pretty right. We didn't get the full points because Heather made me give another answer and officially our answers didn't end up matching, but she was nice and gave him half a point anyway. (And he needed all the help he could get.)

he did. I was on the debate team in high school and I know how to prove my opinion on whatever is the subject at hand. I knew what needed to be said and I was confident that I would absolutely get a unanimous jury verdict in this particular trial. I could win it hands down, eyes closed, hands tied behind my back. I could prove it in essay form, even iambic pentameter if I was asked to put my argument in rhyme. Sounds crazy, right? But I was definitely the girl to do it!

But this time I didn't want to.

This time I didn't believe such a thing to be true. Just because I answered more questions correctly about Howard did not mean I loved him better or even more than he loved me. It probably only meant that I had a better memory for details and facts, that I was a superior test-taker (thanks, Mom!), and that I really cared to know about every little detail I could get my hands on when it came to him because I loved him. Again, I was feeling pretty pleased with my score, and I was just happy that Howard actually humored me and took the test at all because I'm pretty sure that in the past Howard may have been the guy who would have refused to play this game with me, but he didn't. He did it because I wanted him to.

Truth be told, this whole thing was actually a huge victory for me personally, not because I didn't bring up the olives or get upset over Howard's low score, but because these things didn't bother me. I struggle very hard to not "go global" over small silly things. It is Howard who coined this expression about me; I'm a master at taking a seemingly small innocent thing and letting it snowball until I feel like it pretty much means everything. I could assign huge significance to practically any little thing. You didn't bless me after I sneezed; uh-oh, it must mean that you no longer care if I live or die. Yes, crazy, I know. But this time, I wasn't even fighting against the crazy, because it wasn't there. I was able to clearly recognize that the olives and the game results really meant nothing when it came to the state of our relationship. *Phew! It didn't happen.*

To me.

A few days passed and *The Newlywed Game* still wasn't over because I had decided for kicks that it would be fun to open up the contest to all of our couple friends who were interested in playing. I asked twenty-plus couples to play and half responded that they would. Everyone was asked the same questions Howard and I had been asked, and I even offered a prize to the winning couple. The day before all the results were due back Howard and I were in bed talking about it. I was telling him that I was pretty confident that all the women would score higher across the board than the men. (Except for maybe Chris, Mr. Romance himself; for all we knew he could probably manage to score 15 out of 10.) I just believed that women are more curious about such specific details and keep them filed away better too. This idea of knowing someone, or even being known, I think is very important to women. The only way I know how to describe it is that it's mixed in with warmth and security and the idea that we are not alone because someone out there knows our favorite ice cream flavor. Howard agreed, and I did tease him by letting him know that there were already more than a few guys who had scored better than him, but that it was probably because they didn't have such an aversion to tests. *Hey, Howard hates tests the way I hate olives. Awwww, cute.*

This is when I made a big mistake.

It was innocent, I swear, I was not baiting him. I did not

have an agenda (like I will admit I may have had with the whole olive thing that started us on this whole game show odyssey). I said, "Well, at least we could both score perfectly if we had to do it again." And then I repeated the fact that his first kiss was at age twelve and was with Pam Hoberman. I even spelled "Pam Hoberman" to prove that I had it fully committed to memory.

This was met with an odd silence from Howard, and so I said, "What's wrong? Did you not memorize the answer to my favorite singer?" More silence. "You did read what the correct answers were, didn't you?"

"Of course I did, but I glanced at them. I was very busy."

After two years, I now know that if Howard puts up an excuse right away then there is something not kosher in Denmark.

"Who is my favorite singer, Howard?"

He wouldn't answer. He didn't know. He couldn't remember, and he was getting angry. Really, really angry. "I told you I don't like tests."

"Fine." I was upset, but I decided I needed to walk away from this one. It's true; I knew he didn't like tests. He had made that very clear at the bottom of his answer e-mail for the game, where he said that he thought the questions weren't clear enough, that he is not a guy who believes in black and white answers, and that he hates taking tests, especially when under pressure. I had come a long way and I didn't want to blow this now.

But I couldn't help thinking, *It's one thing to not know the correct answers in the first place, but how could he not care after the fact? Did it not mean anything to him that I'm pretty sure if someone asked me on my deathbed who Howard's first kiss was I would be able to say, even if it was my last dying breath, "Pam Hoberman, age twelve, Hebrew camp. She had a great set of . . ."?*

I could feel a stirring inside of me: Crazy had just woken up and was lolling about in its warm bed, but there was a chance it would go back to sleep. *It's not worth it, I thought. I shouldn't have asked. That was stupid of me. We are tired and tense from working on the book. Howard has been working incredibly hard. He was busy. He didn't want to take the test anyway, but he did. Ha, see, maybe he was right. Maybe it was a test. It doesn't mean anything. Remember how when you went to Howard's office to work yesterday he had made you a pink streamer chandelier on his ceiling to welcome you? He knows you like chandeliers and pink streamers!* He had also given me a cute welcoming card with a glittery penguin sitting on an iceberg all by himself and it said, "Where would I be without you?" and upon opening the card it said, "I'd be out looking for you." Who cares that Howard didn't remember my favorite singer? I knew unequivocally that Howard loved me and wanted to be with me. I had no doubts. Not one.

And with that the crazy went back to sleep, and I went downstairs to finish my work.

A few minutes later I heard some noise coming from upstairs (Howard yelling, "DAMNIT," and possibly punching a pillow). Then he came stomping down the hallway and halfway down the stairs. He was angry, really, really angry. He said he felt like I was still testing him—even though he'd told me time and time again how much he hated tests. He felt like he tried so incredibly hard with me, especially lately with the flowers and the card and the chandelier, and like none of that mattered enough to me. That there was nothing he could do to make me see how much he loved me.

I knew how he felt because Howard, if you will, was going global.

I didn't even look at him, but I did put my hand up in the classic stop-in-the-name-of-love sign (sing it, sister, because never was it more true!). And before he could say one word, I said in a very firm and extremely sane voice, "Howard, do NOT make this global. Just don't go there." (In my head I was pleading, begging even, *Please, Howard, don't do it. Just don't. I'm sorry I was so stupid just then. I shouldn't have asked. It was my fault and I didn't mean anything by it. We are tired. We are stressed and emotional. Your back hurts and I know exactly how it feels when all your emotions are swelling up like a tidal wave. Please don't go fully global about this now, because my crazy is a very light sleeper and if you start it, I promise you, I will finish it. And you do not want that. I don't want that. Trust me.*

Strangely, oddly, incredibly, at that moment I also felt a sense of calmness; it was almost like I was happy, because I felt so sane and clearheaded. I wasn't the crazy one. (Though I had been the stupid one for bringing it up.) But I did not want a big dramatic hullabaloo, and I knew how to stop it.

Howard went back upstairs without a word.

He did not finish going global and I never started. We had a somewhat terse discussion ten minutes later where we both explained our feelings to one another. But what Howard didn't know is that I had a very deep understanding of how he felt already. I did. He felt all the exact terrible ways that women sometimes feel when they are feeling crazy and unsatisfied by how they are being treated. And I knew that he felt even worse because his back was probably still bothering him, because he didn't get to stay in his bath long enough. Howard hates it when we argue. All this I understood, and I felt awful that I was the one who made him feel bad because I was a stupid woman.

And what I said to him later was this: "If I had scored only one and a half out of ten, would it not have bothered you even a little bit? I'm not saying it would have bothered you enough to make you feel unloved, nothing so big as that, but maybe just a tiny bit bummed? And then if you found out later that I didn't bother to look at the right answers, wouldn't you say it was like the world's tiniest smallest minutest little kick in the pants of a silly little expectation that you would? Well that's all it felt like to me. Nothing more."

He nodded; we understood each other. Maybe not all the way, but enough to get over it.[5]

---

[5] **Interesting Facts About Our Newlywed/Relationship Game:** The women scored higher than the men eight out of the ten times, there was one tie, and Victoria only scored lower than Jay because she appealed Jay's score and won him some extra points (but not enough to win the game). Jay and Victoria were the only couple that were actual newlyweds.

Tasha and Michael won the game—Tasha scored 7, Michael 4. They have been together for thirteen years and married for seven.

Heather and Eric also scored 7 and 4, but since she was the host and picked the questions she was not eligible to "officially win" (don't worry, she still got a prize). They have been together for a little over three years and living together for two and a half.

Chris scored the highest of all the men. Howard scored the lowest. That Chris . . .

It was a three-way tie at 7 points for the women (me, Tasha, and Heather) but unofficially I scored 9 out of 10 (according to Heather), though I'm not bragging.

Rob and Phil both tied and scored low, which shows that two stupid men are simpatico as a couple too.

Nadine and Paul, when answering how long they had been together both wrote the exact same thing—awww—"23 years. Yikes!" (Please note the exclamation point after "yikes.")

My brother was, like, *really* old when he got his first kiss and I sorta wish I didn't know this about him.

Howard's parents, Larry and Muriel, have been together for the longest amount of time, fifty years by the publication of this book. His brother, Evan, and Evan's wife, Adele, have been together for "a quarter of a century" which just goes to show that the amount of time together doesn't ensure a high score.

Howard and I have been together the shortest time of all the couples, two years, eleven months, and two weeks by the time this book is published. (Which means there is hope for our score yet . . . just kiddin', Howard!)

9

STUPID AND THE CITY

WHAT *SEX AND THE CITY* TELLS US ABOUT STUPID MEN

Last summer, the *Sex and the City* movie opened to "boffo business," as showbiz folks like to say. On its opening weekend it grossed a record-breaking sum of almost fifty-seven million dollars. But Hollywood saw this coming, right? After all, they have what they call tracking, which is like polling, and it tells you how big an audience for a movie is going to be on its opening weekend by measuring the movie's awareness level and "want to see" factor. (It's extremely accurate, except for family films, because tracking kids is harder.) But with adult movies it's right most of the time. The guy who writes the "Movie Projector" column in the L.A. *Times* on Fridays wrote that based on his research, *Sex and the City* would be lucky to make thirty-one million dollars.

It made twenty-five million more than that.

That's a lousy prediction by anyone's standard.[1]

But the L.A. *Times* guy was hardly alone in blowing this one. Damn near every guy got it wrong. Keyword here: guy.

You know who didn't get it wrong? Jenny Lee.

Although she refused to predict hard numbers, Jenny assured me *Sex and the City* would "handily beat" the second week of *Indiana Jones,* which it did, to the tune of *sixteen million dollars.* The prognosticator guys said that a bunch of chicks in their forties could never defeat the mighty Indy. Keyword again: guys.

I, of course, told Jenny she was crazy.

Rationally—if a bit condescendingly—I explained to her the thinking of the guy geniuses: The movie of *Sex and the City* was tracking off the charts with women *over* twenty-five. They were clearly excited to see the movie. But it was not tracking nearly as well with younger women. And it was barely registering at all for men. (Or straight men, I should say.) As for teenage boys, the most reliable and frequent moviegoers, the movie wasn't even a blip on their radar. Without those segments of the audience you've got a "limited-appeal pic," I told her, using the word "pic" to show her how showbiz savvy I was. "You can't open huge with just women over twenty-five!"

"And how many women over twenty-five are there in America?" she asked me.

"A lot, I think," I answered.

"Okay, well, we'll see on Monday then," she said simply, and left the room.

---

[1] I e-mailed Josh Friedman, the L.A. *Times* "Movie Projector" guy, and asked him, "What gives with your SATC prediction?" He wrote back, "I should have listened to Mrs. Projector. That's a recurring problem—just ask her."

And that got me thinking. It did seem like every woman I talked to—though granted, most of them were over twenty-five—wanted to see this movie. And *Sex and the City* certainly has grown in popularity since its origins as an HBO niche show. I mean, my mother watches the reruns on TBS and has become a huge fan. *My mother.* Which would mean even more to you if you knew my mother. As far as risqué programming, Muriel is not the first one you think of tuning in. She's also somewhat of a popular culture snob who takes pride in not knowing what *American Idol* is. But still, even knowing that the *Sex and the City* phenomenon had touched Muriel, *I still believed the prognosticators.* Because they had empirical evidence, right? They had the numbers. I mean, even at its height on HBO it still had a much smaller audience than a network hit. And even if people liked the series on DVD or in reruns on TBS, the original show had ended four years ago! That's an eternity in popular culture. Even the shoes from the original show are out of fashion now. I was with the L.A. *Times* guy. It would do thirty million at best.

I should have listened to my mother.

I should have listened to Jenny and every woman I talked to.

But then again, listening to women has never been my strong suit.

MEN DON'T LISTEN

Here's the thing: Men don't listen to women about things they don't "get." We'd rather complain about what we don't understand than see it from their point of view. The tragedy, of course, is that *it is precisely the things we dismiss that are the very things we should be striving to understand.* (More on that later.) *Sex and* *the City* is not something we get. (As noted, the gay man is an exception.) To us it seems like a comedy with no comedy. A show about sex with women you don't want to see having sex. Everyone is always out to lunch but no one gains any weight. There are all these clothes we've never seen a normal person wear—nor would we want to. And there's shoes and bags and shopping and everyone speaks in puns and there's not much happening in the way of plot. And it's painfully schmaltzy.

This isn't how women see it. They see something completely different.

But that is how it appears *to us.* And that's that, as we like to say, never once stopping to wonder *why* women everywhere love this show. (The *Sex and the City* movie grossed 152 million dollars domestically and *245 million* overseas. For those counting at home that's a total of almost FOUR HUNDRED MILLION DOLLARS.) So when men are stupid about *SATC*'s appeal to women, we're being stupid on a global scale! (But it is comforting to know that our stupidity translates internationally.) But what's more troubling is our often outward disdain and downright contempt for the things that our loved ones love.

I know. I'm an outward disdainer. I'm a downright contempter.

A few weeks ago I was scrolling through our DVR's to-do list with Jenny sitting next to me on the couch. And as I surveyed all the shows she was recording—*90210, Gossip Girl, Grey's Anatomy, Lipstick Jungle*—I actually said *out loud,* "Who can watch this shit?" To which she said, "You do realize I'm sitting next to you."

Men don't have to like *Sex and the City,* but to declare that a woman's love of it is pure folly *is pure folly*—as they might say on *SATC.* If nothing else, isn't it just common courtesy to accept that people have different tastes than our own? And yet, we still feel justified in telling women what morons they are for liking what they like. And guess what? They don't appreciate it. If you agree to go to the ballet but ruin the ballet with your constant kvetching, I can guarantee you one thing: There will be no sex in your city.

THE MORON IN THE MIRROR

FLASHBACK—2001

It all started with Elton John.

Now let it be said, I'm a huge Elton John fan. Ever since Lisa Lasson explained to me in sixth grade how great he was, I've been a believer. I have many of his albums. I saw him at Madison Square Garden years ago, and more recently in Las Vegas. And I will argue with anyone, anywhere, that "Your Song" is the greatest love song of all time. None of which explains what the hell he was thinking with the score for the Broadway musical *Aïda*. Several years ago, I found myself, along with my wife at the time, her sister, and her sister's boyfriend—now husband—at the Elton John/Tim Rice musical version of the opera *Aïda*. They had barely finished the first song and I realized it was going to be a long, excruciating night. (You know you're in trouble when you're actually wishing you were at the *opera* version.) Everything about the production struck me as cheesy and amateurish, from the oversynthesized inane songs, to the *Space: 1999*–like costumes (there's a reference you don't hear very often), to the absolutely cringe-inducing dancing—if you could call it that. Luckily, or so I thought at the time, I clearly had a partner in misery: my sister-in-law's boyfriend, David H. The man who would become my brother-in-law—if for only a few years.

So I'm shifting uncomfortably, rolling my eyes, grimacing in agony, and generally acting like my theater seat is the electric chair. And every grimace, every roll of the eyes, every pained expression is met by David H.'s equally pained look. He starts whispering in my ear a litany of things about the production that make this a low point in a life of theatergoing for him.

Intermission.

The sisters quickly rush to the bathroom line while we hit the concession stand, hoping against hope that Coke and brownies will get us through the second act. We then amuse ourselves by mocking the production and everything and everyone in it. Then we meet up with the sisters.

And here my troubles begin . . .

My ex-wife is holding a CD of the music from the show that she's just purchased.

It turns out both sisters love it. The music, the costumes, everything. They've bought the CD so they can relive memories of it long after we've left the theater. I immediately seize on their merriment. I attack everything about the show, including the people backstage, whom I've decided to dislike on principle. Oddly, my tirade is met with shocked looks, stunned glances, and furrowed, confused brows. My sister-in-law then turns to David H. to ask him how he feels. And without missing a beat, he says, "I love it! It's wonderful! Are you sure one CD is enough? I want one for my car, too."

What?!

The women then gush and coo all over him as they start

talking about how they wish they could break off a piece of Patrick Cassidy and take him home. David H. agrees that Patrick Cassidy is a very good-looking man.

My mouth is agape. "But five seconds ago . . ."

My future and now *former* brother-in-law then goes on some bullshit reverie of how this musical brings him back to the great musicals of his youth. And all my wife-at-the-time can do is glare at me—a too familiar glare. A glare I saw so often I convinced myself it was a glare of love. Turns out it was just a regular glare.

But the damage was done. I was now public enemy number one in her mind. The ultimate killjoy. And boy, wasn't it just so typical of me . . . Meanwhile, the lying sack of shit is wiping up the floor with both sisters! I try to point out that five minutes ago, Mr. Musical Pants wasn't so high on *Aïda*. But it only makes me look *more bitter, more out of touch,* and more inappropriately angry at the "delightful score."

I wanted to kill him. All my ire was directed at the traitorous David H. I made a mental note not to trust him. I was convinced he was the root of all evil.

But here's the thing: He was right.

David H.: one. Howard J. Morris: nothing.

And unfortunately for me, this moment was a precursor of many others to come, where David H. would come down on the right side of what women wanted—and I'd be standing alone on principle on the wrong side. My tirade against *Aïda* served no purpose other than making me look like a giant a-hole. It can't even be justified by *really* being about something else—like when my marriage was truly failing and I was so angry at my wife, I made her friend cry simply because she said she liked *The West Wing*.

It was a dark time.

But this is another time.

A new day for Howard J.

And there is redemption for all of us, if we can actually take what we've learned the hard way and turn insight into action. I vowed to change my killjoy ways. I prayed that someday I would get another opportunity to prove what a positive guy I could be. To channel the David H. within. To be an expert actor on the stage of pretending to love something you don't for someone you do. Little did I know the challenge of all challenges was about to present itself. But was I up to it?

THE *SEX AND THE CITY* CHALLENGE

She got the DVD the day it came out.

There was going to be no escaping the *Sex and the City* movie at my house. She said she really wanted me to watch it with her. (Why? I'll never quite understand. Crazy is my only explanation for why women ever want to do anything with us that they know we won't like. Just this morning she said to me, "That art exhibit I'm dragging you to is getting great buzz." Can't wait!)

But I knew this was my moment.

Perhaps the one I'd been preparing for all of my life. The moment to show that the Howard J. Morris of 2008 was not the same Howard J. Morris of 2001. To show that my love for this woman supersedes my need to be a pain in her ass. And if love means sitting through a little movie called *Sex and the City* without groaning audibly, then I would do so happily. It would be my honor.

"I got the extended version on Blu-ray," she said excitedly. "It's twelve minutes longer! A hundred and fifty-seven minutes total!"

Oh god.

For those of you counting at home: That's a long freaking movie.

I AM MIRANDA

She snuggles up right next to me on the couch and then presses the remote.

Okay, okay, this is cool. Gonna be fun! Here's a recap of the series. That's handy. Oh wow, that's a great apartment . . . You know, I bet he will build her a hell of a closet . . . Jeez, New York hasn't looked this pretty since Woody Allen made good movies . . . Hey, that was a funny line! . . . Look at me, I'm laughing! I can't believe it, but I'm enjoying myself. I really have evolved. I'm proud of me.

She smiles at me. I smile back. We're good.

Oh, this isn't good. She's trying on wedding dresses . . . Lots and lots of wedding dresses. This is a really long sequence of wedding dresses . . . Always good to see current bridal fashions, right? And once this montage is over we'll get back to some plot. It's not like we're going to have any more clothing montages, right?!

She takes my hand and gives it a loving squeeze. I squeeze back. *I'm here for you, baby.*

Oh god, more clothing montages . . . Now all the girls are trying on clothes . . . Oh, look, there's Miranda in a funny outfit from the eighties . . . This is the extended version, huh? Great, more clothes . . .

"It's fun to see them all together again, huh?" she says. "Fun!" I say. But I really sell it. I'm pretty sure she buys it.

Uh-oh, Law and Order is having second thoughts . . . I'm think-

*ing he's going to stand her up at the altar . . . He does . . . Now
she's confronting him on the street and crashing flowers down on his
head . . . Wow, that scene was pretty good. Got some emotion going,
got some conflict . . . Can't wait to see where this is going . . .*

We're going to Mexico.

*She's depressed in Mexico at a fabulous resort . . . Wow, what
does a room like that go for a night? . . . Nothing much happening . . . She's still depressed and one of them is eating pudding . . . The
other one doesn't shave her bush . . . Okay, still in Mexico . . . Still
depressed . . . Oh, no. Did she just say she's in a "Mexicoma"?*

I wince. She notices. I rub my eye as if I have something in
it. She turns back to the screen. Gotta remember to watch myself. If a groan slips out all my good work is for naught.

*Still in Mexico . . . Is there going to be any plot anytime soon?
Something's gonna happen, right? You can't really have a movie
where nothing happens . . . Can you?*

She turns to me with a look that says, "I know what you're
thinking, baby." She then happily explains, "They're living their
lives." As if that actually explains something.

*Okay, back in New York, cool. Love New York in the fall . . . Ten
plotless minutes later and it's New York in the winter . . . Something's gonna happen, right? Hey, where the hell's Law and Order?
Oh, there he is sitting alone on New Year's Eve . . . Oh, look, there's
the talented girl from American Idol . . . Now it's spring, something's gonna happen now, for sure. Oh no, they're going to Fashion
Week. It's not . . . no, it can't be . . . oh, god, no . . . it is . . . another
clothing montage!*

My head drops.

I didn't mean for it to drop but drop it did! A chin-meeting-
chest, can't-take-another-clothing-montage kind of drop. While

I was guarding against the unintentional groan and the eye-roll *I forgot all about the head drop!* I prop it right back up, but she notices. Big time. "Okay, you don't have to watch it," she says, not angrily and almost sympathetically. And I'm tempted to take her up on her offer, I really am. But I know that if I go upstairs and watch *The Shield*, I'll never be that guy she wants me to be who doesn't rain on her parades. I'll get a "Good Effort" instead of an "Outstanding," and it won't be the same black mark on my record that *Aïda* was, but it won't signal much progress either. "No, no," I say honestly, "I was just a little thrown by another clothing montage." "But you have to see the spring fashions!" she says, as if this were obvious and lucky for me that she pointed it out. "Right!" I say. "The spring fashions!" Though not in the convincing way of a great actor, but more in the desperate manner of a man who's holding on for dear life. I take her hand and focus again on the screen. But her hand is tentative and limp. She's having doubts about me and this whole endeavor, I can tell. I grip her hand firmly and fix my gaze on the runway and Samantha and Charlotte. Finally, I feel her hand clutch mine as before. I peek over and see she's lost in her delight again.

I've made it back from the head drop.

It's a place few men have ever come back from.

Now if I can just make it through the next hundred minutes . . .

I'm going to focus on the positive! I'm going to find things to like, that's what I'm going to do! Hell, I'm going to suck the joy off the screen! Hey, this movie is so long that I don't have to worry about what I'm going to do for the rest of the day! That's good. And you know what? That Mario Cantone is one funny gay guy. Funnier than the other gay guy, who I don't think is gay in real life . . . I like Evan Handler, too. I re-

*member seeing him in many plays in New York in the eighties. I won-
der if he's ever going to say anything. He's been in a bunch of scenes
but they don't seem to want to let Evan Handler talk . . . Oh, here he
is talking in the hospital scene! There you go, Evan! It's your big scene!
Wow, that was over quick . . . Speaking of New York in the eighties, I
remember seeing Cynthia Nixon in a play with Josh Hamilton at the
Young Playwrights Festival and she was fantastic. I had a total crush
on her. This was when she was blond and before she was gay . . . Hey,
remember when Cynthia Nixon was on Broadway in two shows at the
same time?* She did Hurlyburly *with* William Hurt, *then went down
the street for her scenes in* The Real Thing *with* Jeremy Irons, *then
managed to get back to* Hurlyburly *for her curtain call.* Hurlyburly,
*now that was a long play. Was that play as long as this movie? Hey,
I wonder if I can still understand what's going on in the story if I just
watch the left-hand corner of my big screen . . . Yes, I can!*

She nudges me. What? What's happening?

*Oh, look, they're at city hall and she's laughing with the girls!
And Law and Order is there! Now they're eating at a diner . . . Now
they're drinking cosmos . . . The credits roll! It's over!*

I made it.

Or did I?

What's the verdict? She looks over to me and smiles. But
what does the smile mean—other than she loved the extended
cut? *Oh, god, she's not going to ask me to talk about my feelings
about the movie, is she?!* (A week ago, she asked me which character I thought she was most like. I was at a loss to say the least.
"Amanda . . . ?") Oh, god, what's she going to say?!

"I feel like you should get like a good boyfriend certificate
in the mail or something." She smiles.

Yes. Victory.

WHY THEY LOVE IT AND WHY IT MATTERS

As I said before: *We openly dismiss the very things we should be striving to understand.* When Jenny Lee first came back from the movie, she told me, "It was kind of like an overlong episode where nothing much happens." "So, it sucked, huh?" I said. "Oh my god, I LOVED it! I can't wait to see it again!" she squealed. *Why?!* "I just love the characters so much, it was good to catch up with them."

Women are just different from men.

For one thing, they're better at loving than we are. And more loyal. Even when they give their affection to *made-up characters,* it's unwavering. And the relationship between the audience and these particular characters is a passionate one. (And there's nothing women like more than a good relationship!) So while we're waiting for something to explode, they're having a relationship with the characters on the screen. Interestingly, men also know a thing or two about being passionate fans. Consider the insane way we feel connected to our sports heroes who thrill us and torture us in equal measure. I could make a case that our Manny Ramirez is their Samantha Jones. But the point is not to understand it in our terms *but to understand it in theirs.*

You don't have to like what your crazy chick likes, but to not *want to* understand it is insanity. It signals an inability in us to reach across the aisle, as the politicians are fond of saying—or more importantly, to reach out to her. Yes, we're talking about intimacy here, guys—the thing she craves and the thing that gives you a headache just from hearing the word. But the more you can understand the world *outside your own,* the greater your ability to connect to her will be. And your ability to love in a way that's bigger than yourself, in a way that's truly meaningful *for her.*

She has to do the same thing for you, of course. She has to reach across that same vast divide to reach your world. *But women usually do and men usually don't.* And this makes women crazy. And for us *not to do it* makes us irredeemably stupid.

Recent news reports announced that they're planning a sequel to *SATC.*

Start making those cosmos, guys.

JENNY'S RESPONSE

CRAZY AND THE CITY

I have seen every episode of *Sex and the City.* Twice. First when I was living in New York City in my twenties (it was the only night you'd find me home watching TV—this is pre-TiVo). And then at the age of thirty-four, when I returned to New York after leaving my husband of almost five years, who had made the unfortunate error of moving me to Boston right after we got married. When I watched the entire run of the show straight through for the second time it was a totally different experience because I was now the same age as the girls on the show, and I loved it even more. I, too, could now call myself a warrior when it came to looking for love, finding love, losing love, getting married, getting divorced, and being back to square one. Trust me, being in your thirties in the city is very different from living there when you're in your twenties. (More credit card debt, because you have more expensive tastes, and you absolutely get that boys will come and go but your female friends will always be around.)

One of my all-time favorite episodes of the show is when Miranda's mother dies and she has to buy a bra for the funeral and ends up crying in the arms of the saleswoman. It really touched me because it highlighted one of the best parts about living in a huge urban city, which is those moments of connection with strangers that make you feel part of something larger than just your own microcosm of existence. It's those Blanche Dubois–depending-on-the-kindness-of-strangers moments that always show up right when you really need one that make you understand that we are all in this together. Now, seven-odd years later, I had my own random emotional reckoning in a bra department of my own city.

You never think you're going to be that girl, the one who confesses her sins to a lingerie saleswoman, a perfect stranger, but there I was in a dressing room in a Beverly Hills department store doing just that. She was fitting me for a bra that would hopefully be perfect for the dress that I was going to wear to a wedding in a week. I had forgotten to bring the dress to the store, so we were just winging it and hoping for the best. While she walked through the racks and pulled bras for me to try on I followed her like a little lamb and just kept talking.

I spoke in a low and reverential tone. "I just saw the most awesome boots in the world." She eyed the extra large shopping bag slung over my shoulder. "Okay, I bought them. But it happened so fast. It was like I was possessed." (In my head I could see the lighted movie marquee: *Zombie Shopper 3: The Boot Possession.*)

She smiled politely because her job was to help me find a bra, and nowhere in her job description did it say that she had to subdue a crazy customer hellbent on confessing her most recent shopping sin.

"My boyfriend's going to kill me. Like dead." (*Zombie Shopper 4: Her Boyfriend Killed Her—AGAIN*, no marquee on this one as it was a straight to DVD release.) Again, she didn't say anything, but she did give me her best sympathetic we've-all-been-there-honey-and-this-too-shall-pass look.

This would have been the appropriate time to just let it go, but as I obviously had gotten into this dilemma by my overall lack of restraint, like a freight train I continued full speed ahead. "So the question is, do I tell him? Or do I hide them in my closet? Oh my god, I can't believe I'm that girl who is hiding shit in her closet. I don't want to be that girl. Sure, I've accepted the fact that I'm the girl who buys things and keeps the bag in the trunk of her car until I'm sure I made the right choice, but I'm not a hide-it-forever-lead-a-double-life-of-fashion type." I comforted myself with the knowledge that just because I was considering hiding them in my closet, I wasn't technically that girl, until I actually hid them there . . . yet. Right?

"Ugh, should I just tell him the truth?" As I asked this I did realize I could just have easily asked whether I should return them while the receipt was still warm in my wallet, but I wasn't ready to go there yet.

Finally she spoke, probably realizing it was the only way she was going to get me to shut up. "Even if you tell him he won't understand." It was obvious by her matter-of-fact tone that was all she had to say. She then showed me to my dressing room and told me to call if I needed anything else.

That was all I got. (I guess my moment of crying in the arms of a random saleslady in the dressing room wasn't going to happen, well, at least not today.)

As I began to try on the bras she picked out for me, I couldn't help think about what she said. Shopping is always and will always be a very complicated issue between men and women, and so I was fascinated by her direct one-liner approach. By saying that he would never understand even if I told him, was she saying that there is no point in telling my boyfriend about the boots because he wouldn't understand anyway, and so therefore it would be a futile endeavor and I should just hide them? Or was she just trying to impart some larger and more profound truth: Men don't understand shopping period.

As much as I would love to flag this topic as yet another area in which men are stupid first, thereby causing women to be crazy second, I believe it's more fair to admit that when it comes to shopping the craziness starts with women. (Though men freaking out about it after the fact is stupid because it's only going to exacerbate an already emotional situation, and might cause women to go down the road of being secretive and cagey on the topic.)

I wondered if it were even possible to get a man to understand how a woman feels about shopping, especially as most men seem to shut down at the first sight of a shopping bag. But if we convinced them to listen to our story of how it came to be that we ended up with a new pair of sunglasses when we already owned several pairs could they ever understand? I thought about the boots and decided I would be better off just telling Howard the whole story.

In my defense, I knew right from the beginning I shouldn't

have bought them. I wasn't even the one looking for boots, well, I guess as a woman, we're always looking for boots, but I swear I wasn't actively in pursuit of boots that day. It was my friend Zander who was looking for boots. She was then writing on a hot new show with a bunch of fashionable lesbians and she suddenly found herself in want of motorcycle boots. I teased her that she was obviously succumbing to subliminal lesbian peer pressure, because nothing is more butch chic than motorcycle boots.

Anyway, so there we are looking around and I'm dutifully pointing out every cute boot that Zander might like, and then . . . I see them. They were stunning. A matte black, buttery leather knee boot, split down the middle on both sides but held together by crisscross leather straps that encircled the boot and then buckled jauntily on the top at the side. The pictures that fired in my brain were a field of tulips, ballet slippers, and the last scene in *The Shawshank Redemption* when Tim Robbins finally escapes from prison and he's holding out his arms in a state of pure bliss. I just couldn't believe it; I may have finally found the perfect pair of boots to fit my fat calves! (I've always had a fat calf issue when it comes to boots. It's sort of my dirty little shame secret. I just can't wear a lot of the tall fall boots because I can't fit my calves into them. Sad but true.)

So Zander picked up one of the boots, looked at the price tag, and shook her head no, no way. I threw my hands up in the air; what was she thinking? One should never ever look at the price first! So I'm like, that bad? She's like, even worse than that. Being a good friend, she made me look. Ouch. They were expensive. Crazy expensive. Walk-around-the-sanitarium-lawn-in-your-bathrobe, paper-slippers, and-dirty-hair expensive. She motions for me to keep moving and under no circumstances was I to touch them. I take a breath; she's right. We move on. We see a pair of Miu Miu ankle boots that have some very cool buckles and Zander is tempted to try them on, and in my head I'm chanting silently to myself, "Try them on. Try them on. Try them on." It was my hope that if she tried them on I would then have an excuse to try on the strappy boots in an act of girlfriend camaraderie. Friends don't let friends try on shoes alone. But she stayed strong, and refused. I was sad, but I knew it was for the best.

Besides, I was broke. I wasn't even writing very much lately. The economy had gone to hell. I DID NOT NEED TO BUY ANY BOOTS. NOT EVEN BOOTS THAT WERE OBVIOUSLY CREATED BY GOD HIMSELF. Zander and I were now in the cosmetics department and I was thinking about buying myself a lipgloss as a consolation prize. (Sorry that you didn't win your dream boots today, but at least your lips will be shiny when you're crying yourself to sleep tonight.)

When it was time for Zander to go don't think that she just left me there like a bulimic in a cupcake store, no, she checked in with me to make sure it was okay for her to go. I assured her I was fine. I was. The plan was to completely avoid the shoe department, finish my other errands, and then get the hell out of Dodge. Just start driving west until those boots were a distant memory behind me.

I'm lying. Well, not totally. The noncrazy side of me, which isn't so much a side but more like a few aberrant brain cells, was all for the plan of ignoring the boots. But the other side of me, the real me, knew I was powerless not to go and see them again, but I was afraid. Afraid they might be even better than I thought they were. And afraid that maybe they weren't the boots that were going to change my whole life (I actually already owned a few pairs of those), but maybe they were the boots that were to *be* my whole life.

As soon as I reached the shoe department, I saw him.

We were two strangers whose eyes locked across the crowded dance floor. The music seemed to pull us together and we met right next to THE BOOT. Looking down at me he asked, "What size?" As if he was asking me to dance. I almost blushed and gave him my best "Who, me? You're asking me to dance?" look and I replied, "I'm a size thirty-eight." I was powerless to say no, and I couldn't even blame it on the fact that my corset was laced so tight it made me lightheaded and unable to think straight.

I sank down on the cushiony couch and waited. I was Cinderella. No, I was Cinderella before she even knew she was Cinderella. I was just one of the thousands of girls who happened to be in a shoe department of one of the thousands of department stores across the country who was hoping to find her glass slipper. Just praying that I would receive the knock on the door that I would open to find the king's men standing there presenting me with the magical boot that could possibly change my life as I knew it forever. "What? I'm actually a princess? Really? How fabulous for me."

I looked over, holding my breath, shyly and demurely at the display boot again, and I imagined one of Cupid's arrows going straight into my heart. Bull's-eye. Everything became clear, and I knew that if these boots were drowning in a lake I would risk my life to save them. I would fight the current, the wind, the waves, the floating debris, the sharks and killer whales, the undertow (fine, so there is no undertow or sharks or killer whales in a lake, but whatever, just go with me), and I would swim and swim and dive and dive until I saved these boots from a cold and waterlogged fate (god, to think what water would do to such beautiful leather; it's too terrible to imagine).

When he arrived with the big boot box I sat up very straight. I was nervous. I was giddy. My mouth went dry from the antici-pation and I was licking my lips like a girl on coke waiting in line to get into a disco where she will meet her future husband to the beat of the early Madonna song "Burning Up."

They fit. Not just in a regular way like "Oh, they seem to be about the right size." No, they fit like I was born thirty-seven years ago in Nashville, Tennessee, for the sole reason that I would be living in Los Angeles in 2008 to try on these boots. As if every single experience I had in my life was to get me to this exact place at this exact time. It was like I was the main character in one of those choose-your-own-ending books where you get to the end of the page and it says, "If you choose to go to the dance with Jimmy, turn to page twenty-seven, or if you choose to join the chastity club in high school, turn to page thirty-eight," and you knew that by turning to whatever page you chose the course of your life and the ending of the story would be totally different.

This is the part where the movie fashion montage starts: The latest Pink song begins to blare and we see me, a very skinny movie-montage version of me of course, all decked out in leather pants, wearing these boots, walking down a street in Paris; we see me in skinny jeans and a plaid shirt taming a wild stallion on a New Mexico cattle ranch wearing these boots; we see me wearing black spandex sequined tights with a gor-geous silk organza poet blouse wearing these boots, and I'm dancing on a stage with Archie, Veronica, and Betty. (Hey, it's my montage and if I want to dance with cartoon characters to "Oh Sugar" you can't stop me.) We see me wearing these very boots when I am sprinting out into traffic to save the life of a small child who is chasing a puppy. I save both of their lives by the narrowest of margins, just missing getting squished by a big semi truck, and later when I'm being interviewed for the evening news for my heroic, selfless deeds the first thing out of the female news reporter's mouth is "Awesome boots, where'd you get them?"

Ugh. There was no chance in hell Howard would ever understand. He's the guy who hates fashion movie montages when they don't further the plot of the movie. I could hear him in my head: "Your montage is all over the place dramatically. Animation? Really, Jenny?"

The bargaining stage was fast and furious. I'd be hypervigilant on my diet. I'd work on my writing like a house on fire, day and night. I'd plant a tree and recycle more. I wouldn't be so stingy with cookies for my puppy. I promised that I'd just be a better person in general if only I could just have these boots.

This is when I remembered my emergency credit card.

"Emergency credit card" meaning that I'm a girl who once had massive credit card debt and was no longer to be trusted carrying credit cards at all, so now I just had one card that was for, well, emergencies. (Sure, I had a card that was my boyfriend's, but I knew that buying the boots on his card would basically be signing on the dotted line of my own death warrant.) This credit card hadn't been used in two years. It was for emergencies only. Emergencies like getting kidnapped; escaping out of a dirty, dark basement; and having to get myself home from

Cairo, where I had been sold into slavery to make those little ceramic spoons with the different states on them that people collect from those convenience stores found at rest stops along the highway. This credit card was not an emergency fashion credit card (though god, what a great idea that would be), but again, it was a card strictly for the purpose of life-or-death and weird sold-into-slavery scenarios.

I thought about leaving behind my boots. (They were already mine in my heart, and I knew that even if I didn't get them and some other woman bought them they would still always be mine.) I thought about how if I left them behind it would be like leaving a little piece of myself behind with them. In fact, I wondered whether that little piece I left behind would actually be the piece that could lead to my death. (We're not talking the appendix, tonsils, or a second kidney, we're talking a major vital organ. Like I could die without them.) I'm not saying that I actually believe that, but it felt like it could be true.

That settled it. It was life and death. And it was now up to me to give myself a happy Hollywood ending or a sad tragic one. And damned if I was going to live my life like one of those sad indie movies that not only refuse to give you a happy ending but pointedly give you the crappiest ending imaginable. I knew what I had to do. I handed over my emergency credit card.

If I had been a guy it would have been a classic stupid move, and I would definitely have been accused of not thinking. But I'm not a guy, and the only thing I was guilty of was thinking too much about them. The crazy had taken over. Every feeling and every emotion I just relayed was the whole truth and nothing but the truth, so help me shoe god. It's exactly what happened step by step: so what if it was all just in my head, that didn't make it any less real, did it?

When I was paying for my new bra, I had trouble meeting the saleslady's gaze. She's the one who had gotten me started thinking about all of this in the first place, and as much as I wanted the *Sex and the City* ending, her suddenly channeling SJP and reassuring me that it would all work out, I knew that I was going to have to face the music alone.

I was tempted to tell her that I had decided to tell my boyfriend the truth about the boots. How it was an emergency, and that it had basically been a life or death situation. Of course I already knew what his response would be: "Basically life or death? Really? So you're saying you were basically about to die over these boots right here? And you give me shit over misusing the word '*ironic*'?!"

Hmmmm. . . . So maybe that wouldn't work. Maybe I'd tell him that when we lose our home after he bails me out of debtors' prison we would be thankful that we live in such a warm climate and that sleeping on the beach isn't as bad as it sounds. Maybe I could tell him to leave me in debtors' prison. I'd be fine. I'm personable so I know I'd make friends. Or I could just run away to a cool climate, somewhere that I could wear my boots year-round. Or even just drive over to Zander's house where I knew she would gladly let me be a fugitive in her guest room. I wouldn't even have to explain anything to her. She'd see the bag and just direct me upstairs.

Okay, maybe I was blowing this whole thing out of proportion. I mean one thing I had in my corner is that as far as boyfriends go, I had one that was pretty open-minded. He was a writer after all who understood the drama of real life. In fact he watched the *Sex and the City* movie with me just a few days earlier. The extended version. And he didn't fall asleep. (But he had wanted to kill himself.) So it's not like my crazy shopping story would come sailing out of left field for him (or is it to left field? Out to left field? Would end up in left field? See, look at me getting better with sports analogies). I'll just tell him to think of it like I have a sickness, and today I happened to have a particularly bad case of it.

But then I thought about the price. How big his eyes would get when I told him. (Even if I rounded down they would still sound expensive.) The trick was to find the most sympathetic metaphor. If only I could get a doctor's note to say that a little piece of me would have died without them. (Though if it wasn't the little piece that controlled blow job function I'm sure he'd be fine with it.)

I never said anything more to the saleslady about the boots. She just thanked me for my purchase and wished me luck with the rest of my day. This made me feel better. Sisterhood is never more powerful than when it comes to shopping. And I knew she wanted me to have my happily-ever-after-in-fabulous-boots ending. I knew this, because I wished the same for her.

On my drive home I gave myself a pep talk. I could do this. It would all be fine. If he said, "What were you thinking?" I now had at least fifteen different metaphors to try out.

When I got home he was all cranky and tired and watching football. I quickly decided that it wasn't the right time. After all, he saw me walk in with a lot of shopping bags, but he didn't ask any questions. And I didn't give him answers because clearly I didn't have any.

It occurred to me that if I did tell him the whole story I was running the risk that he would not only find me crazier than he originally had me pegged for, but he would also think me stupid. I couldn't afford the boots. I didn't need the boots. I certainly shouldn't have bought boots that could adversely affect my current relationship. What the fuck was I thinking?

The morning after not telling him, I read his chapter "Stupid and the City," and I saw that he was a man who was really trying hard to understand something that he may never be able to understand. It seemed like he got it a little bit, but I guess we won't know until he reads this, my own private episode of *Sex and the City* (the Jenny Lee story), the episode about the boots. Yeah, that would definitely be the final exam for men everywhere. Is it possible to really understand how women think about shopping? So it's decided. I'm going to let him read this, and that's the way I'll let him know that he doesn't have the same girlfriend as he did only one day ago. Yesterday, I was just the regular old crazy-like-a-fox me; but today I'm the crazy-like-a-fox me but with awesome new boots.

And yes, I promise to add an epilogue of what happened after the fact—well, if I'm still alive then.

EPILOGUE

All you have to know is that he got halfway through the chapter before it all clicked into place. He stopped reading and looked up at me. "Wait, you *bought* them?" I wasn't sure what to say, because, duh, yeah, that's what the whole story he was reading was about. Of course I bought them.

"Are you mad?" I asked. He shook his head and just finished reading. The first thing he said was, "It's really good. Of course, you don't see me having to *buy something* to write a chapter." The sarcasm was to be expected and I grinned and bore it. Hell, I deserved it.

"Are you mad?" I asked again. He said no again, but this time in a way that showed he was definitely mad.

"You're mad, I can tell." But he kept denying it and I let the subject drop before I found myself instigating a fight that I myself really wanted to avoid.

But trust me, he was mad. And how I know it, and how I know that men will never be able to fully understand what goes on in a woman's head when she shops—even though I just wrote five thousand words that explained it in every glorious psycho detail—is very simple.

He never even asked to see them.

Seriously.[2]

---

[2] Women who are reading this and would like to see a picture of the boots, please send me an e-mail at crazyjennylee@gmail.com, and I'd be happy to e-mail you a picture. And once you see my awesome boots feel free to write Howard and tell him what you think at stupidhoward@gmail.com.

10

EMPATHY FOR THE NUT BAG

FEELING HER PAIN

Today wasn't just any stupid day in my stupid life. Today I was *special* stupid. I was "Sir, you've just been inducted into the Stupid Hall of Fame" stupid. The previous night I'd gotten back from a week-and-a-half stay in New York, and this morning I arrived early at my office in Santa Monica, ready to get back to work on this book. But as I was going to park my car, I suddenly became enraged to discover that someone was parked in my spot. Not stopping to think—why would I? I never have before—I screech my car to a halt, thus blocking two other cars from *their* spaces. I barely find time to turn off the ignition as I jump out of the car and bolt upstairs to see Melanie, the mild-mannered mortgage broker who parks next to me and works in the office below mine, to ask her if she knows anything.

Melanie knows something.

She tells me that the car has been parked in my spot for

about a week or more and it hasn't moved. Melanie wonders if it's been stolen and abandoned there. I'm with Melanie. Something nefarious is clearly afoot. So together, we call the building owner/manager, Larry, who's sick as a dog and sounds like he's dying on the speakerphone. Larry suggests, through his coughing and phlegming, that I put a sign on the car explaining that this person is parked illegally and will be towed. Then even mild-mannered Melanie gets riled up: "The car has been there for a week and a half, Larry! No one's going to see the sign!" She knows that Larry is just putting off taking any real action, and then repeats even more adamantly her suspicion that the car has been stolen and abandoned in my parking spot.

I start to wonder, with the subprime mortgage mess and all, whether this isn't in fact the best part of Melanie's day.

Larry hems and haws and wheezes that he can't deal with this now and please put the sign on the car. I say, "Fine, I'll put up the sign. But I still have no place to park and it's not gonna do a damn thing!" And then with real manly moral-ground venom, I add, *"This is your responsibility, Larry!"* The infirm Larry hocks up a lugie and finally relents. If I put the sign on the car he will call the police. We hang up and Melanie hands me a piece of paper for my sign. My frenzy is even frenzier now. My handwriting shakes on the paper. "YOU ARE PARKED ILLEGALLY," I start to write. Did I spell "illegally" right? Melanie's not sure, she's a mortgage broker, not an English teacher. Then I start fantasizing about the nasty things I'm going to write on the sign. I'll show this person just who it is they're messing with.

Melanie, meanwhile, like the dogged but ever polite Inspector Columbo, once again muses about how *odd it is* that the car has been in my spot for a week and a half and I've been gone that long, so she just assumed it was my car. *But it's clearly not my car,* I tell her, *since I was driving my car, and I only have one car!*

Uh-oh. Terrible sinking feeling. Oh no . . .

It's *not* my car. *It's Jenny's car.*

(Before we left for New York, it was Jenny's very considerate idea that we park her car in my office parking spot, so that our house/dogsitter would have a place to park in our garage at home—and wouldn't have to troll the streets late at night in search of parking.)

I'm having my girlfriend's car towed.

Larry calls back to say a tow truck is on the way, and he's going to call the police. *What the hell am I going to tell Larry?!* I just insisted that a man near death get the hell out of his sickbed to take care of his angry, righteous tenant!

I hem. I haw. I start wheezing and coughing but I'm not really sick like poor Larry. Melanie then jumps into action. She yells into the speakerphone, "It's no problem, Larry, we figured it out! The car's being moved right now!"

"What are you [cough] talking about? Who the hell [wheeze] was [phlegm clearing] parked in his—" *"Don't worry about it, Larry!"* She hangs up on him.

Saved by Melanie. A woman I barely know.

I sink into a chair, now trying in vain to crawl up into myself and hide from me. "You didn't notice it was her car?" Melanie asks sweetly. "It was dark," I utter lamely. "I only saw it from the back for a second . . . I just . . . *reacted.*" A man's instinct is always to rage first, then apply reason later. Luckily, a woman's instinct is usually to protect that same idiot. Melanie saved me this time. But I've been saved so many times before by so many other women. And she didn't do it because of some fantasy that my father invented the paper clip and I was heir to a great fortune, and she'll now be rewarded with riches beyond reason and never have to deal with this mortgage mess. She saved me because she had empathy for me. She knows what it's like to be mortally embarrassed and wanted to spare me that fate. A simple act of kindness. A simple act of *empathy*.

Jenny reacted with equal amounts of charity and forgiveness when I told her the gruesome details later that morning. And I was trying to tow *her* car! But in Jenny's case, she knows that my sound and fury most often signify nothing other than my own frustration with myself. I find that women in general seem to understand that men just lose their shit sometimes. And when we do, something is always thrown, or hit, or crushed into little bits. When a man is faced with the inevitable truth that he is indeed small and insignificant, despite all his efforts and vows to the contrary, he starts kicking a car, or pulls up a root of a vegetable he's just planted, or decides to "clear the kitchen table" as Marlon Brando did in *A Streetcar Named Desire*. And when a woman sees this a tiny part of her dies inside. But incredibly, women are made up of *many, many* tiny parts.

It's called empathy. They feel our pain.

And what do we do? We shit on theirs.

To be blunt: Men suck at empathy. We're almost as bad at sympathy, and that's the easy one. All sympathy requires of us is to *intellectually* understand how someone might be feeling and to accept it. We don't even have to feel anything ourselves for that one! But women want more. Empathy is the big kahuna of emotional responses. And it's the one we don't give back in any way that measures up to the way in which it's given to us. And this bums women out. Big time. And it makes us seem very, very stupid to them.

But it's tricky.

Women insist that in order to feel their pain we don't have to, say, crap out a watermelon to simulate the pain of childbirth. But I'm not so sure.[1] Men ask: How can I feel something if I don't feel it, don't understand it, and have never felt anything remotely like it? But somehow *women do.* And that's what they always say: "We do it for *you.*"

Here's what I understand about empathy: You really have to put yourself in a woman's shoes, or high heels, or those cute sandals from Neiman's she wants. You have to *listen* to her feelings, *respect* them, and, whether you understand them or not, somehow *relate* to them. (This is the toughest part. You have to really get under the hood for this one.) But in relating to her pain, you can't bring up *your* pain, because her pain is *her* pain, and it's not *your* pain—even though you're supposed to be feeling her pain right along with her.

Does anybody see how we might have a problem with this?!

I didn't get empathy at all until I had a son. Because when a baby falls down and starts wailing, you instinctually know what to do: You hold him—never a bad thing with a woman either—and you speak as soothingly as possible. *"Yes, I know it hurts, I do. I know, honey. I know. I know, baby. If I fell like that I'd be crying twice as hard. You are so brave. You are such a brave*

---

[1] When faced with crapping out a watermelon or dealing with a woman's feelings I'm not so sure most men wouldn't opt for the watermelon.

little boy. Yes you are! Yes you are!" But who can't relate to falling down and hurting yourself?! That's an easy one to have empathy for. The problem men have with women is that they want us to have empathy for their *feelings.* No matter how insane! And frankly, women have too damn many feelings. Who can keep up? They're like feeling anthropologists, discovering new ones you've never heard of and rediscovering ones thought lost to previous generations. We have trouble with the basic ones and now we're being asked to empathize with the fancy, elusive ones. I once heard on the radio that the average woman knows the names of over three hundred and fifty colors. The average man knows *eight*. It's the same with feelings. We're outnumbered and outgunned before we can even get our first "Oh, baby" out of our mouth.

For this reason many men rebel against this idea that we too must be empathizers. Some men think empathy is for sissies. Hell, woman! We can stop that irritating noise the toilet makes when it won't shut off after all your jiggling of the handle has gone for naught! Why the hell do we need empathy?!

"Because that's how people feel loved, dipshit," is how it was once put delicately to me.[2]

STUPID MAN, FEEL MY PAIN!

After Jenny and Melanie's generous responses to my imbecilic behavior of the morning, I vowed to try much harder at this

---

[2] Full confession: I am not one of these men who can make that toilet sound stop. I can barely change a lightbulb. So I guess I'm completely out of excuses for not actively pursuing this empathy thing.

empathy thing.[3] I certainly acted like a nut bag. So how could I not have empathy for one? I wanted to really put myself in Jenny's mind-set as much as I could: to not just see things from her point of view, but to really *feel* them. I could hardly wait for the next opportunity I got to empathize, to offer compassion, understanding, generosity of spirit, and to not judge.

I immediately had a test of my Emergency Empathy System.

I had come back to Los Angeles from New York while Jenny had stayed on the East Coast. She took the train up to Boston to reconnect and spend some time with a former love: her old dog Wendell. Wendell isn't just any dog, he was the dog love of Jenny's life. She wrote a hilarious and moving book about him called *What Wendell Wants: Or, How to Tell If You're Obsessed with Your Dog.* She had custody of Wendell for the first two years after her divorce and the dog has been living with her ex-husband in Boston since she moved to Los Angeles.

On the phone, Jenny told me that the reunion with Wendell had gone extremely well. He totally remembered her and was as excited to see her as she was him. *Great,* I thought as I breathed a sigh of relief. Frankly, I had been none too empathetic about her desire to see Wendell. I just didn't really get what the point of it was. I knew that she felt terrible being three thousand miles away from him, missed him desperately, and really wanted to make sure he was all right and was being taken care of properly. But I just figured seeing him would cause more unrest than any

---

[3] Even Jenny's decision to park her car at my office was an act of empathy. For our dogsitter. Jenny hates having to find a parking space—which can be near impossible where we live. And not wanting the dogsitter to feel that frustration, especially when dealing with our dog, she made sure the dogsitter was taken care of. It's also empathetic to our dog, who she doesn't want to be cared for by someone who is stressed out and harried. There's no end to her empathy!

kind of resolution. With her ex-husband clear that the dog was staying with him, wasn't it better, I wondered, to let sleeping dogs lie in Boston? But now that she'd actually seen him, she did seem more at peace and less fraught about the whole thing. I finally understood why it had been so important to her.

My empathy was on the rise, I thought.

Then she told me that she and Wendell were staying the night together at the Charles Hotel.

"The Charles Hotel?"

"Yeah, it's really nice here," she assured me.

"I know it's nice. It's like one of Boston's best hotels!"

Oh, empathy, don't desert me now.

Why couldn't they just stay in the park and play some more? I wondered. She wanted more quality time with him. After all, they had a lot of catching up to do. And she didn't come all this way to just see him for a few hours and split!

"Holiday Inn, anyone?" I asked.

"Only certain Holiday Inns take dogs," she said. "And Wendell will be more comfortable at the Charles."

It's hard to dispute that. The Charles Hotel actually has a "Doggie Stayover Package," which includes "an overnight bag with bowls and *organic* food." There's also an extra sixty-dollar cleaning fee—and not because Jenny has a tendency to poop on the furniture. So fancy people stay at fancy hotels with their fancy dogs all the time! It's not outrageous at all! "And seriously," Jenny said, "it's not like we're staying at the Ritz."

"If that dog orders a porno on pay-per-view I'm gonna be pissed," I said, my tone veering a tad toward the sarcastic. I thought the Charles Hotel was excessive and wasn't shy about mentioning it. And I repeated my concerns (key phrase: *my* concerns) about this whole reunion. I imagined Jenny and Wendell in their hotel bathrobes the next morning having to say good-bye and fretted about the emotional mess Jenny was sure to be. And of course, while not saying it overtly, I'm thinking, *Oh god, what if her ex-husband actually relents and gives her back the dog? Then we'd have another dog—which is a lot more work of course—and what if her old dog doesn't get along with our dog, Doozy?!* And I was off and running in my own head about my own crap. (The thought never crossed my mind, of course, that Jenny got an actual human being as part of the package when she moved in with me.)

At this point my empathy score was sinking fast. (But my boorish self-centered score was taking off!) She hung up the phone in that way people do when they really want to kill you but are trying to suppress their murderous feelings at least for the moment. But the true shame of it all is that I should have known better.

Empathy with her situation wasn't even a reach for me.

PUPPY LOVE

One thing I used to be really stupid about—and equally un-empathetic about—was how intensely people love their dogs and how special a love it is. I just didn't get it. I scoffed at dogs. I didn't have one growing up. And nothing irritated me more than when someone brought up their dog as a legitimate topic of conversation. I was one of those people who, upon finding out that a friend's beloved pet had died, would comfort him by saying, "Hey, it's not like a real person died." I was *that* guy.

Then I got one.

And everything changed for me at age thirty. It took all of three minutes for me to get the whole "man's best friend" thing. I loved my first dog, Maggie, with an almost lunatic and obsessive intensity. I found myself thinking about her when I wasn't with her. Was she happy? What was she doing? And I bawled like a colicky baby when I had to put her down eleven years later, as I had when her younger brother, Doc, died unexpectedly. Jenny and I have a dog right now, Doozy, that we both absolutely adore. Dogs just make your life better.

And I know a little something about leaving dogs, too.

When I got divorced Maggie and Doc stayed with my ex-wife, who had a backyard and a lifestyle more conducive to taking care of them. But when I finally left the house that July morning, I remembered the night six months earlier when I'd come home to find that my wife had moved into the second bedroom. A house already filled with drafts had just gotten chillier. But the dogs slept with me that night and for every night thereafter, Maggie taking her place dutifully curled in a ball at the end of the bed, only her neck jutting forward to rest on my ankles, and Doc, who we always called Mr. Trouble and who couldn't seem to get close enough, doing everything he could to sleep *on top of me*.

They were true friends at a time when I needed some.

Still, when I stepped out of the house that day and into my new life, I actually felt relief at not having to take care of them every day. These were high-maintenance Labradors after all, and I had a baby boy to make a second home for. But soon after, I realized that for all my complaining about taking care of the dogs, they'd really been taking care of me. Imagine, all that time spent thinking I was walking them, only to realize they'd been walking me.

MEN ARE STUPID 213

Later that night, I had an empathy spasm.

I e-mailed Jenny and said I was sorry about my self-centeredness, and I told her that of course her old dog was welcome in our home, and, said, "If you need help smuggling Wendell back to the West Coast I'm all in." She told me later that my e-mail made her cry. Unfortunately, not that "he really loves me" cry, but the "where the hell was this when I needed it?" cry. You can't play catch-up in the empathy game. You have your shot and if you miss it, that opportunity is lost forever.

FAKING ORGANIC EMPATHY

Since then the subject of empathy has been a big one in our house. And last night Jenny told me that she didn't want a man who faked empathy. She wanted the genuine thing, the real article, or no empathy at all. But I'm not so sure that's true. More than one man has heard a frustrated woman cry, "You could at least *try* to have a little empathy for me!" Isn't *trying* in this case a *kind of* faking? (And I mean "faking" in the best sense of the word: like faking an orgasm!) Jenny wants us to *try* but to not *fake* it, but what I really think she means is: If you have to fake it, fake it *well*.

But at least we do have a role model, a master of the empathy game whom we can learn from. A man for whom the term "a gift for empathy" seems to have been invented: Bill "I feel your pain" Clinton. No matter what you think of Clinton's politics or character flaws—and Jenny's not high on Bill for his infidelities, which she takes as a personal betrayal—there is no denying that Bubba is the empathy king. And whether it's calculated or organic, or, as I suspect, a blend of both, we can all learn from him.

HISTORICAL MOMENT IN EMPATHY

The first George Bush, by his own admission, lacked what he called "the vision thing." What became painfully obvious in a defining moment in his failed reelection bid against the young Bill Clinton was that he lacked "the empathy thing." In a moment in their town hall–style debate in Richmond, VA, the elder Bush bungled a question from a woman so badly, while Clinton's answer was so brilliantly empathetic, it is considered today to be a major turning point in the election. Empathy proved beyond Bush's reach—as was a second term in the White House. (It's required YouTube viewing for any guy who doesn't want to get thrown out of his own house.)

A woman in the audience asks the candidates how the national debt and the mess of the economy has affected them *personally.* Clinton is listening to her intently—all wide-eyed empathy. George Bush is *checking his watch.* (In fairness, he might have had a dentist's appointment he was late for.) But think what would happen in *your* house if you checked your watch as soon as your wife asked you about your feelings on a subject she was clearly affected by. It wouldn't be pretty.

But wait. It gets much worse.

At first—incredibly, for a Yale man—he doesn't seem to understand the question. "The national debt affects everybody," he says petulantly. But then the moderator and the questioner both say, "*You.* How has it affected *you* personally?" The woman then tells him how it's affected her: She knows people who are losing their homes, can't make their car payments . . . Still nothing. You can see his mental mouse clicking but nothing's coming up on the screen. *He just can't grasp that all she wants to know is that he understands her.*

So naturally, he does what all men do when terrified of a woman's emotions: He tries to argue her out of her feelings. (I guess because *that* always works so well.) "Are you suggesting that people of means aren't affected by the national debt?" he says haughtily. Defending rich guys. *There's* a surefire way to a poor woman's heart. Then, seizing his misguided moral high ground, he practically demands an apology *from her.* "I don't think it's fair to say that just because you've never had cancer, you don't know what it's like. I don't think it's fair to say, uh, you know . . . whatever it is, if you haven't been hit by it personally . . ." So he's not actually *being* empathetic but defending his *right* to be empathetic—if only he had feelings like normal people do. He goes on to say a jumble of words that seem like English but don't actually make any sense when put together. Finally, he admits he didn't really understand the question at first but thanks her for clarifying it.

Then it's Clinton's turn.

He makes a beeline for the woman, and what's the first thing he does? He says, "Tell me how it's affected *you* again." She's tongue-tied for a minute and startled to see him so close to her. "Um . . . ," she says nervously. He puts her at ease. "You know people who've been laid off?" She nods yes. "I'll tell you how it's affected me," he says directly. And then he goes on to say that he's a governor of a small state and he's seen up close the very real effects the government's inaction on the economy has had on people's real lives. He then tells her, "In my state, when people lose their jobs, there's a good chance I'll know them by their names. When a factory closes I know the people who ran it. When a business goes bankrupt *I know them.*"

What is he? Governor of a shoebox?! How could he possibly know them?! Arkansas is a small state but it still has three million people! *But the facts matter less than the feelings of empathy that he's conveying.* It's the tone, the warmth, the sincerity, the concern, the connection, and not least of which, the *effort* he's making to comfort her that makes her not question how he knows everybody in the world who's been down on their luck lately. They may be from different places but he's telling her, *I know you're hurting because I hurt too. And I want to be there for you.* And wherever she's coming from he's going to meet her *there.* It doesn't matter how long the drive. And he's not checking his watch because he'd rather be somewhere else.

Let's review George Bush's attempts to win this woman's heart: checks his watch as she starts to talk. Can't seem to understand the word "personally." Gets defensive. Defends rich people. Deflects all emotion by getting technical. Then accuses *her* of not being fair to *him.*

He's a real catch, this guy! If only he had a son!

NOW OR LATER

Here's another way for men to look at it: Empathize now or pay later.

Because if you mess up this empathy thing, you're going to be the guy who finds himself, later that night or the next, in one of those tortuous, endless conversations in which you're sorting through her deep feelings. And you're going to be asked repeatedly why you can't be there for her *emotionally* the way she is for you. And it's going to go on all night long. And you're going to be trapped there wondering if you'll ever see daylight again.

I bet you can empathize with *that* feeling.

Here's what happened later with me and Jenny: Having failed in my stated goal to be more empathetic to her after the "car towing incident," I knew I had to try again, as it became clear that my lack of support for her visit with Wendell and for her desire to get him back was really upsetting her. So we sat down on the bed and I braced myself for a long and bumpy night.

I did not check my watch.

I did not defend my previous behavior.

I did not accuse her of not thinking about me.

I did not bring up me at all.

I did not bombard her with practical considerations.

I let her talk about everything she was feeling without interrupting.

And then something actually happened to me.

Maybe it was the result of working from the outside in, but all of a sudden I was focused completely on her, and I could really feel the pain she was experiencing over the loss of her dog and how terrible it must be to not feel supported in that. Then, like a man obsessed, I snapped into "Let's get Wendell" mode and listed a bunch of different options for approaching the subject again with her ex-husband. She considered all of my new ideas, but more importantly for her, there was something she sensed in me, some truthful bit of empathy toward her condition, that seemed to calm her down. She told me she felt much better about us and the whole matter in general.

I don't know how the situation with Wendell will ultimately resolve itself.

But we got to bed before twelve thirty.

(Not that I was looking at my watch.)

JENNY'S RESPONSE

A NICE LITTLE B-AND-B FOR SHANE

After I finished reading Howard's last chapter I found myself shaking my head. Call me a cynic, but I never thought he'd make it this far. It's nothing personal against Howard, of course, it's more that in all my past dealings with men (I'm including my friends' dealings with men as well) I've just determined that where women have a glass ceiling, men, it seems, have a stupid ceiling, and it's doubtful whether they can break through it. Sure, you can condition them to buy more flowers, to read grocery lists better, and to even try their best to be more empathetic and better behaved, but they will still always be men. And believe it when I say that is exactly what we want, because we do not want men to be like women.

In fact, even though I would never want to switch and be a guy, I have to admit there are times when I envy their simple, seemingly stupid ways. Yes, empathy doesn't come naturally to them and they have to work at it, but my crazy cup overflows with it. So much so that I find myself often tired from treading in the deep waters of my overabundant emotions.

So now Howard's face is pressed up against the glass window (or the stupid ceiling, if you want to continue with that analogy) and he's so close his breath is fogging up the glass. And all I can think about is whether I should help him break through. I feel the urge to protect him, to tell him to "run don't walk" away, and to sit him down and tell him a cautionary tale of the scary things that go on in crazytown. "Oh, Howard, you may think you want to visit, but you would never want to live here."

I believe that shows like *Grey's Anatomy,* movies like *Steel Magnolias,* and even soap operas serve a purpose beyond just pure entertainment for women. They are actually helpful in relieving women of some of their excess feelings. So when we get too fraught and emotional, we have to curl up on the couch and watch chick stuff just so we can emote it all out of our system. It's like how you always feel better when you are pent up and you just cry it all out. Women are like sponges and we just get too full (which makes us crazy), and watching Meredith and McDreamy try to make things work while saving lives actually wrings us out, in a good way. Howard finds such shows and movies to be manipulative and cloying. But I think he doesn't understand them because they run on such a high empathy frequency that only girls and dogs can hear.

But though he may think that women only empathize with TV and movies where someone's dying—like four Southern women who hang out together in a beauty parlor—he's wrong. Women empathize with anything and everything, even sports. Men have a favorite team and they just want them to win. Period. Women have favorite teams that they want to win, too. But they also always empathize with the losing team. I always ask Howard whether the losing team cries in their locker room after the game. He finds this question annoying because he doesn't want to think about it. Sports are about winning and losing; you pick a side and just let the chips fall where they may. If your team wins, you are happy. If your team loses, you are sad. That's it. But in my head I always picture the losing team's locker room being filled with a bunch of guys sitting on benches with towels over their heads, crying over their disappointment at not winning the game and maybe even calling their moms.

Howard tells me I shouldn't worry about the other teams, but I can't help it. I think about their wives and girlfriends who are now also upset and worried about how they are going to deal with their moody husbands and boyfriends when they come home. I worry about the parents of the players. I even feel bad for the coaches and their families too.

To further exemplify this idea I'm going to tell you how I feel when I watch *The Shield*, an award-winning cop drama with a loyal and very male following that can easily be called one of the most macho and masculine shows ever. It follows the lives of a group of cops on the wrong side of the law who do not abide by the morals of our society, but instead live by their own personal honor codes that seem to say that as long as they are standing on the heads (sometimes literally) of the villainous gangbangers and murderers and drug dealers, then they're doing okay—that being a good cop sometimes requires breaking the law yourself.

The show is dark and violent and one could say the extreme polar opposite of a chick show like *Grey's Anatomy*. Good hair is not only not celebrated in *The Shield*; it is of no concern to Vic, the antihero, because he has no hair. (And even if Vic Mackey had hair, you know he wouldn't care about it. Howard thinks that McDreamy is just a guy with good hair who knows how to cry.)

Howard has been a fan of *The Shield* since the beginning, and I have only just started watching it with him this year. And I can easily say that I am watching it mainly to share the experience with Howard, not for my own enjoyment.

Here is how Howard watches *The Shield:* First he takes off his pants because he likes to watch it in his boxers so his own "detectives" can breathe. He needs a blanket around him because the extra security is comforting when the gritty realism gets to be a little too gritty or too real (and he's prone to getting chilly). He needs it to be totally dark because the show is not filmed in HD, so he needs to make up for it by not having any other light sources to bother him. He needs total quiet, so there is no talking or unwrapping of candy while watching *The Shield.* If you think you are about to cough or sneeze or breathe too loudly, you must stealthily grab the remote and hit pause. And if you must go to the bathroom, then you should go beforehand. *The Shield* moves fast and requires his full concentration. Howard does not hold my hand while watching *The Shield* because, well, Vic wouldn't give a reason, so why should he? And that's it, he's in. He watches with undivided attention and all he is thinking about is what's going to happen next.

This is me watching *The Shield:* I'm engaged but also a little stressed out because Howard is so tense, which makes me tense. Sure, I want to know what's going to happen next, but in the pie chart that is my brain there is a lot more I am concerned with. It doesn't matter that you've never seen *The Shield* before and that you don't know the characters; what I think about and empathize with has little to do with what's happening on the screen.

I wonder why Dutch isn't married; he seems like he'd be such a sweet and gentle husband. He really should worry less about that potential serial killer kid and focus on why he doesn't make time for a girlfriend. He really seems like he'd be such a good boyfriend. Maybe it's because he loves Claudette and he is depressed because his love is unrequited. Dutch has such creamy skin and he obviously uses sunscreen. I wonder what brand he uses? I doubt as a cop you would spring for the fancy stuff, but maybe it's his one indulgence. Maybe he takes a little bit of pride in being the cop with the great skin—as smooth and white as alabaster. Poor Claudette, it's gotta be so damn difficult to get ahead in such a male-dominated world. I wonder whether she ever thinks about growing out her hair. She might be thinking that the short haircut gives her a look of more authority. Does she know Dutch loves her? I wonder if she doesn't share his feelings because of race, or because he's younger or has better skin, or maybe because she's his boss and doesn't want the other cops to make fun of her. She looks tired. I wonder if she likes to eat pancakes when she gets home from work, which is what I like to eat when I don't feel well. Why is Vic so damn angry and tough all the time? It's like he gets off on living on the edge of a high-rise building, but he should watch Oprah and learn he has other choices in how he could live his life. His ex-wife looks like one beaten-down broad. I hate to use the word "broad" but that's what he has made her into. Having Vic as the father of your children really must suck. And she knows he's a bad guy too, which must make her sad. I wonder if she wishes she had never married him or met him, or wishes he wasn't born. Oh, but then she wouldn't have her kids, so probably not. Her youngest two children have autism. That's really a difficult situation. I wonder if she's read Jenny McCarthy's book. I wonder if she wishes Vic could be more like Jim Carrey, who has so obviously bonded with Jenny's young autistic son. I'm glad that Jenny and Jim seem so happy. I wonder if they are going to get married. I wonder if Vic cares that Corrine hates him. He has such a big ego and it's like he feels entitled to her loyalty. He exploits her weakness, which is that she wants her kids to have a relationship with their father (and though he won't win any father awards it is obvious that he loves his kids).

How terrible to have such a soft spot for a guy like Vic. His daughter on the show looks a lot like him and Howard told me she is actually his daughter in real life. That's sweet. I bet she's happy to be working with him. I wonder if they ride to work together or eat lunch together. What is up with Ronnie? I like Dutch the best, but I sort of like Ronnie, too. I would set up Dutch with my friends, but I would like to live next door to Ronnie. I would bring him soup when he is sick and tell him that he should stop bringing home hookers and find a nice girl from a local nail salon to settle down with. (Ronnie likes Asian girls, and there's a cute manicurist who works at my nail salon who I think would be perfect for him . . . if he were a real person.) I wonder why Ronnie is so damn loyal to Vic. Ronnie looks too thin in his dark suit. He shouldn't wear a black tie, only undertakers should wear black ties. Undertakers and Regis Philbin. But not Ronnie. It's sad that Vic and Ronnie and Shane are all fighting. It's tough to be at odds with your best friends. They were once so close, a happy foursome in their clubhouse that they cutely call "the barn," and then Shane killed Lem. I wonder if I ask Howard which guy corresponds with which girl in Sex and the City whether he'd break up with me. I bet he would. Shane killed Lem, and now Vic and Ronnie can't forgive him. Poor Shane. Shane had an affair with this underage black prostitute; it was sorta sweet how he fucked her in abandoned buildings. It's like he really cared for her, and she was totally in love with him too. It's nice when people find someone they can connect with, even if it's against a dirty wall of an abandoned crack house. Shane's wife Mara is very pale, has a lot of freckles, and is a little too Lady Macbeth-ish, which is why Shane was in need of sweetness from his young junkie prostitute. Mara is definitely a woman who needs a bubble bath, or a month at a spa, or a free subscription to O magazine. She is just so angry all the time, but I do think she loves Shane even though he's *a major fuckup. He shouldn't yell at her so much. Now that Shane and Mara are on the run they have had some very tender and romantic moments. Because they seem so happy and are having these very sweet and very un-Shield-y moments I bet one of them is going to die in the last two episodes. I think it'll be Mara, because it'll be more poetically tragic that her own cop husband couldn't shield her from death. I bet Shane will cry and cry if that happens. But maybe if she dies he'll have a second chance to start over. Maybe he can find that hooker girl—she's probably finished with seventh grade by now—and the two of them could run off to Mexico together. Maybe they could open a charming little bed-and-breakfast by the ocean. She could learn to cook, and he could learn to fish. Now wouldn't that be nice . . .*

Oh, it's a commercial. I wonder what's going to happen next?

In the show Mackey's wife, Corrine, always had her suspicions that Vic was involved in some pretty bad stuff, but when it all finally came out into the light she asked him in all seriousness, how could he do it? How could he do all those terrible things? (In that moment Corrine was representative of all women out there asking their husbands why they did the dumb-ass things that they did.) And in all seriousness Vic replied, "I didn't think about it."

There will always be a divide between men and women because we're different. Men sometimes don't feel enough, but women, sometimes we feel way too much. It would be nice if there was a happy medium, a place that you could visit every now and then that is in between *Grey's Anatomy* and *The Shield,* a place where the grass is always green and maybe you could stay in a cute little B-and-B that is run by an ex-cop and his ex-prostitute girlfriend.

11

CRAZY LOVE

It was my first tooth.

It was my son's fifth that he'd lost, but incredibly, the first one at my house. Being a divorced father has given me knowledge and experiences in many new areas but I was a Tooth Fairy novice. Until now. On tooth five. I needed to pump him for information quickly. He was already putting the tooth under his pillow. I feigned casual.

"So, uh, what happens when you lose a tooth?"

"The Tooth Fairy comes."

"Right. So the Tooth Fairy leaves what, like five bucks? What's a tooth going for these days?"

My son looks at me, confused. "The Tooth Fairy doesn't give me money. She always leaves me a present."

Okay, a present . . . *She couldn't just give the kid a few bucks like every other mother in the world?*

"And it's a very special present," he tells me.

Okay, very special . . .

"And it always comes with a long poem that the Tooth Fairy writes about me."

Great!

"And it rhymes."

She's clearly getting me back for the deer thing.

"And it always comes on pretty paper—"

"Go to bed!" I say a little too loud.

He climbs under the covers and looks up at me. Then, to my complete surprise, he starts to question whether the Tooth Fairy really even exists. After all, he's just turned seven and he's been around the block a few times—it's where the Starbucks is—and he's having some major doubts. (I have to admit, I'm more than a little tempted to blow the whole thing—shove a few bucks under his pillow and call it a night.)

He knows tonight is the crucial night.

Because if the Tooth Fairy can find him at Daddy's house, then the Tooth Fairy can't be Mommy, right? (Mommy is, if not his chief suspect, then at least "a person of interest.") But if that same Tooth Fairy, so consistent with her special presents and long, rhyming poems, finds him here—a good ten-minute drive away from Mommy's—then he'll know the Tooth Fairy is real.

At least for one more night.

A little more magic. Just for a little while longer.

I kiss him good night.

As I head downstairs I'm wondering where the hell I'm going to get him a present, let alone a long poem about him that rhymes. I can't go out and get the damn present because Jenny is working late and leaving children alone in the house at night is generally frowned upon. (Even if they are sleeping.) I have no other choice but to try to bang out the poem. But the more I labor the lamer my attempts. I'm having trouble finding the

Tooth Fairy's voice. I'm no dainty sprite. But even worse, I can't rhyme for shit. I just don't have the gift.

Roses are red. Violets are blue. You lost a tooth . . . and so did you!

And now it's getting too late to go to a toy store. What "special present" am I going to get him at Rite Aid? Divorced-dad guilt envelops me. I'm not just ruining the Tooth Fairy for him. I'm going to destroy all fairies—forever. I picture him waking up the next morning and flinging his Peter Pan book at me. *"And don't even talk to me about that bitch Tinkerbell!"*

For my son there will be pixie-dusted dreams no more.

And then Jenny Lee walks in.

(I know she *must* have walked in. But as I see it now in my mind's eye, she flew in through the window, wand in hand, wings spread and fluttering, and landed gracefully in the living room.)

"You gotta write this stupid fucking poem!" I scream at her before she can even catch her breath—she's worked late, remember, and hasn't eaten dinner. But that doesn't stop me from assaulting her at the door with my incomprehensible rantings. "You have to write this! I got nothing! It's from the Tooth Fairy! And I gotta go out and get a present!" I go to grab my coat and head to the door. She bids me to slow down. I explain the situation and then calmly she tells me that I should relax. She has plenty of presents she can give him "from the Tooth Fairy." Huh? We're going on a car trip in several weeks and she's *already* picked up a bunch of toys and stuff to keep him occupied for the long ride. That's incredible! We have the present! No hunting for *fun toothpastes* at Rite Aid! I can stay home!

Note: Jenny Lee is always extolling the benefits of planning in advance, preparing for every eventuality. I always think she's neurotic, and frankly, *crazy*—always obsessing about contingency plans for scenarios that are never going to happen anyway. But who's the lucky winner tonight?

Oh no. We still have the poem.

"Fine, I'll write the poem," she says without a moment's hesitation.

"It has to rhyme."

"It has to rhyme?" she says, the first wrinkle forming in her otherwise smooth brow.

"Expletive, gerund, ex-wife's name," I say.

She immediately goes over to the computer and sits down at it. I figure at most she'll write two or three lines that seem Tooth Fairy*ish* and we'll have dinner. But that's not Jenny Lee. That's not how Jenny Lee rolls. Jenny Lee is an A student. Jenny Lee tries harder. Jenny Lee was first violin in high school even though she didn't have Sandy Chin's natural talent. Jenny Lee doesn't do anything halfway. Jenny Lee does not *love* halfway. And Jenny Lee will be damned if my boy's innocence is going to be lost on her watch.

And Jenny Lee is crazy.

She does not stop working on the poem for two and a half hours.

The woman is starving but refuses all food. And there she is slaving over a poem that will most likely be cast aside a moment after it's read, sure to play second fiddle to the Etch A Sketch or whatever it is she got him for the car trip. I plead with her as one hour turns into two. "It's just a fake note from a false fairy!" But she'll have none of it. She's not going to let this kid down. Or more significantly, she's not going to let *me* let my kid down. And she sweats over every word as good poem-writing fairies will. The words do not come easily but they finally do come. And when at last she gets up from her composing on the computer, she takes a piece of stationery and painstakingly writes out her poem in the perfect cursive that only a pixie could have.

When we finally sit down to eat dinner at ten thirty, I ask her why she did it. She says simply, "Because I love you."

> In the very sunny state of Cali
> Where I was flitting about the valley
> I heard my tiny alarm bell ring
> Which never fails to make me sing

This is the divine madness of women: They choose to love us.

> There's a little boy out there
> He lost a tooth but it's been found
> I show up when his sleep is sound
> I whisk it away to my castle high

From that very first moment on the playground when we shove them in the mud puddle, they look up at us and think, *This is the guy for me!* It just gets worse from there but they only become more steadfast in their determination to love us.

> Up, up, up, I must fly
> I check my book, I find his name
> It's Dustin Morris of Santa Monica fame
> Now it's time to think, I know just the thing
> I grab my big silver bell and give it a ring!

As grown men we say we "purple" them because we're too lame to say the word we really mean. We cross a crowded room to sit next to them only because they're sitting near the non-pareils. We say the stupidest possible things at the stupidest possible moments—like in bed after sex. We don't understand anything they like and tell them they're crazy for liking it. And we're always raging against the dying of the light—or when someone's in our parking space. *We try to have their cars towed!*

And they love us, still.

> *Ten silver swans go swimming by*
> *And then all at once they get up and fly*
> *But behind they leave a present or two*
> *The perfect thing to bring a smile to you*

"I'm crazy for trying and crazy for crying, and I'm crazy for loving you."

Patsy Cline might have sung it, but Willie Nelson wrote it—a man so stupid, it should be noted, he didn't know he had to pay taxes—but Willie knew exactly what he was really telling all the girls he'd loved before: Of course you're crazy. *You would* have *to be crazy to love us.*

> *Have fun, be brave, always be good*
> *I wish I could stay, I would if I could*
> *But I'm always around, I'm always quite near*
> *I've got the best job, I bring joy and good cheer!*

They see what's *in us.* And they love us anyway. We see only what's in front of us. And often we miss even that. If you did a love/benefit analysis on the average relationship, you'd find that we benefit and they end up in analysis. And it's not like they didn't know it going in. Everyone warned them: "You're crazy for loving that guy!"

We are all that guy.

The next morning my son still believes.

LOVING THE CRAZY

Don't be the guy who doesn't see it.

Women's Number One Complaint About Stupid Men:

He's too stupid to see what he has in me.

To paraphrase an old movie advertisement: "If you're only going to stop doing one stupid thing this year, stop doing this one *first.*" Don't let your woman's number one complaint about you be "He's too stupid to see what he *had* in me."

Little boys see it.

They see the magic as clearly as they hear the ringing of an ice cream truck bell. I can tell from the way my son looks at Jenny, and at his mother, and even more tellingly, how he looks at that crazy girl in Hebrew school with the *High School Musical* barrettes who talks more than a mile a minute. (Wearing a Little Miss Trouble T-shirt, no less.) He gets quiet, shakes his head, smiles stupidly, and can't take his eyes off her. Then the next day—apropos of nothing—he brings up "that crazy girl who talks so fast." He already understands that there's this special magic that *only exists* inside these strange foreign creatures. Not to say his pal Lucas isn't a cool dude and great at Wii baseball, but his friend Gemma definitely has that indescribable, game-changing, tongue-tying magic.

Now, of course, he's too young to comprehend any of these complex new feelings, and I know what that means: My little boy is already off on his stupid journey with women. I have to admit, I get a little misty eyed thinking of him shoving his first girl into her first mud puddle . . . Perhaps I can guide him through some of the bigger stupidities sure to come. (Of course this is always a parent's fantasy, I suppose.) But what can't be ignored is the *pureness* in the way he sees what we as grown men *stop* seeing: their magic.

Don't be the guy who loses sight of what little boys see.

Women are magical. They're special in a way that we're just not. They love better and love harder and they make our lives greater in a million ways every single day. And for better and often worse, their magic is *inextricably connected* to what we commonly view as their insanity. To put it another way: **The magic is the crazy is the magic.** And to deny that, to try to rid her of that, is only to rid her of herself. And eventually all she'll rid herself of is *you*. You can't separate the crazy from the chick. And you wouldn't want to. Because you'd lose the magic, too.

And the same goes for the stupid man.

Our very hardheaded stupidity can also be our greatest strength in life *and* in love. A lot of our so-called "stupidity" or "simplicity" is actually just a guy being able to blow through a lot of trumped-up neuroses and see the unvarnished truth for what it is. Our stupidity fuels our loyalty, our desire to have you at any cost, and our determination to take care of you. It also makes us a lot easier to fool! And unlike men, women can trust that their thoughts are safe: We will never read your mind. If a woman tries to obliterate what is a major part of her man, it's just going to end badly for everyone. It's like Olive Oyl telling

Popeye, "I dig the bulging muscles, and thanks for saving me all the time, *but for godsakes, can we have corn tonight?*" It's Lois Lane telling Superman, "Enough with the flying everywhere, can we take JetBlue for once? You can watch CNN on the back of the seat in front of you!"

Trying to make someone into someone they are not always fails.

Then what the hell's the point of this book?

(I know women got it by page two, but let me just spell it out anyway.)

The truth is as it always has been. And there is no miracle on earth that will ever change this basic fact: **Women are crazy. Men are stupid.**

This book has been about the gentle nudge.

The gentle nudge we can lovingly give each other and *give ourselves* toward the other—to find that place we know exists between us but don't go to as often as we'd like. The place of love and calm and respect to be found somewhere between total whack job and complete imbecile. But this can only come from changing *our own* behavior—or at least checking it out in the mirror every once in a while. If we can bring men and women just a little bit closer to understanding each other and where each is *really* coming from, maybe we can all feel just a little less alone.

And never underestimate the power of the gentle nudge. Especially the one we give ourselves to see things from another point of view. You'll be amazed at all the things you just might see that you didn't know were even there.

Hell, you might just find out that your girlfriend is the Tooth Fairy.

JENNY'S RESPONSE

ROMEO, THY NAME IS HOWARD

As many headaches as a stupid man can give a woman, he can also give as much joy. My intention in cowriting this book was never to grumble and complain and laugh at stupid men, but rather to celebrate and marvel and laugh with them. Without their stupidity where would we be today? I know one thing: We certainly wouldn't have the greatest love story of all time. If you really stop and think, Romeo could have been more sensible and just looked around for a note from Juliet, or even just stopped to think the whole thing through before he killed himself so damn fast. And, upon waking, I'm pretty sure the first thing that Juliet thought when she realized what happened was *You stupid, stupid boy,* and I bet her second thought was *Wow, how wildly romantic that he couldn't live without me and took his own life!* And when she followed his lead for real this time, she would cement their place in couple history as one of the first examples of crazy and stupid in action. I mean, who is crazy enough to drink some weird potion that will slow down her breathing and almost stop her heart just so she appears to be dead . . . really, Juliet? Did you really think your plan was a good one?

But when we look at Romeo and Juliet now, we never focus on their insane and idiotic actions; we only see the love and romance.

Looking back to the beginning of my relationship with Howard, I see it as hilarious and romantic, and it was, but it was also a good preview of what was to come in the future. As a woman, you always remember the very first dumb thing your guy did. Well, this was his: We had been working together for five months already and though we both really liked each other personally, neither one of us was viewing the other as a romantic prospect. Howard was too busy running the television show he had created. And my biggest roadblock was that he was my boss on my very first job in television, and sure, I'm crazy, but I'm not stupid. So when Howard called me in a panic on a Sunday afternoon, having lost the outline on his laptop that would one day become the backbone of my very first credited television script, I didn't hesitate, and I told him I'd be at his house in twenty minutes to find it.

I found the missing document and then we proceeded to work across his dining room table for two straight hours until we were interrupted by a phone call from his brother. After he finished the call he asked whether I would like a tour of his town house. He and Dustin had been living there for almost one year, and it screamed "divorced dad," meaning there was nothing on the walls, little furniture, and candy wrappers on the floor (which I had the feeling weren't necessarily to be blamed on Dustin).

All I really remember of the tour was that one of the three second-floor bedrooms was empty except for a chair, but his plans were to one day turn the room into a library, which would also discourage overnight guests. And on the third floor there was a small loft space that overlooked the master bedroom and had two balconies. Outdoor space in Southern California is obviously not a rarity, but to me it was a very big deal. (At the time I was subletting a small apartment in West Hollywood; it had an actual orange tree outside my window that I couldn't stop talking about to my East Coast friends.)

Standing out on that balcony together, it suddenly began to feel like we were at the end of a first date and the inane conversation that he was making was just him being too nervous to make his move. I wouldn't say I started to panic, but I was the one who suggested that we go back downstairs and finish our work so I could leave. You see, I wasn't sure if this "kiss moment" was really happening or if it was just me being crazy. But what I did know for sure was that this was not a first date, and the last thing I wanted was to become a future *60 Minutes* special about the perils of interoffice dating.

When we were downstairs I nervously asked to use his bathroom and it was there that I gave myself a stern talking-to in the mirror. I reassured myself that it was all in my head, that it was the balcony and the fact that it was dusk that made the moment upstairs seem romantic, and that we were just two people who worked together who also happened to really like one another as people. That's all.

When I walked out of the bathroom I saw Howard sitting at the table, which is when we FADE IN:

(Welcome to Hollywood. Please note the following script is how it actually played out; there was no artistic license used, and I can honestly say I couldn't have written the whole thing better myself.)

INT. DINING/LIVING ROOM—EARLY EVENING

JENNY, 35, enters the living room from the foyer bathroom. HOWARD, 42, is sitting at a glass dining room table. Jenny takes a seat across the table from him.

HOWARD: I think we have a problem.

JENNY: What? No, we don't. Trust me, we totally have the Sherman story.

HOWARD: That's not the problem.

JENNY: Oh?

HOWARD: I think I want to kiss you. Is that a problem?

JENNY: Uh. Well. I, uh . . .

HOWARD: Let me ask you something. If you were me, what would you do?

JENNY: Oh no you don't! I'm not falling for that one!

HOWARD: So what should we do about the problem?

JENNY: Well, I, uh, we could . . . I dunno, maybe we should make a pros/cons list?

With a FLOURISH, Howard flips over a piece of paper that is on the table in front of him. He grabs a pen and quickly scrawls PROS/CONS LIST.

HOWARD (as he's writing): Pros: It would feel good, WANT TO, you're pretty, like you, good hands, good girl, don't think too much. Cons:

> awkward at work, you're neurotic (as
> am I), we work together.

He puts down the pen.

> HOWARD: So now what do we do?
>
> JENNY: Well, normally, I think a de-
> cision is made based on the number
> of pros versus cons, but I don't know
> if that will work in this particular
> case. Those are some pretty big cons.
>
> HOWARD: True.
>
> JENNY: But . . .
>
> HOWARD: Yes?
>
> JENNY: Well, seeing that we are
> both so neurotic, perhaps we
> should . . . we could kiss and see—
>
> HOWARD: Because it could be horrible.
>
> JENNY: Exactly.

Feeling relieved, Howard then writes "could
be horrible" under "Pros."
    Then, HOWARD SLAMS down the pen and MARCHES
around the table and TAKES JENNY in his arms
and KISSES her. WOW. IT'S A DOOZY OF A KISS.
After several beats they break apart and
stare at each other.

> HOWARD: That was—

JENNY: Not horrible.

HOWARD: Definitely not horrible.

Howard takes the pen and writes "NOT HORRIBLE—CON." He then UNDERLINES and CHECKMARKS it twice for good measure.

HOWARD: Now what do we do?

JENNY: We could finish the outline?

HOWARD: No. No more work.

JENNY: We could make out on the couch for twenty minutes, but no clothes are coming off. Okay?

HOWARD: Done.

FADE TO BLACK.

I saved the original pros/cons list that Howard wrote down that night (October 1, 2006) and it is now framed along with the script that you have just read. It is hanging on one of our walls in the very town house where I was once a guest but now call home. (This is just one of the few things we now have up on the walls. We also have furniture, a library, and a blow-up bed in the garage for overnight guests.)

If you analyze what happened, you can see that Howard's first stupid move was that he wanted to discuss our first kiss before we even had it. Second, I was totally joking when I suggested that he make a pros/cons list, but he stupidly did it anyway. And last, he didn't do the smart thing, which would have been to follow his own pros/cons list; instead he stupidly ignored it, even though the cons clearly outweighed the pros. Three stupid moves in quick succession, one tremendous kiss, and I was his. Sure, sometimes stupid moves get you stuck sleeping on the couch, but sometimes stupid moves get you a chance to make out on the couch. A few months later his stupidness put on its cape and saved the day again, as he staunchly refused to accept my crazy logic when I was trying to break up with him solely based on my own fears of getting hurt sometime in the future.

That night I had it in my head that we just didn't have a chance for a future, and how I explained it was that there were ten thousand ways that this relationship wasn't going to work. Relationships are complicated, we're both complicated, the timing was complicated, we both have very strong personalities, we're both writers, both divorced, he has an ex-wife and a child, I technically didn't even live in California, and seriously, how did we possibly think we could make this work?

My arguments were emotional and made no sense at all, and Howard could easily have crossed my craziness off his list right then and there, but he didn't. He stupidly dove into my little sandbox of quicksand and just started saying the stupidest things.

"Whatever you're afraid of happening has already happened."

What is he talking about? What does that mean? That doesn't make any sense.

"Yes, you're absolutely right, there are ten thousand reasons why this relationship might not work out."

Is he agreeing with me even though I'm not making any sense? Wow, he's dumber than I thought.

"We have to find the one way that works."

Is he telling me what to do? Or is he implying that I don't know what I'm doing? What's he going to say next, that I'm being crazy?

Somewhere during those next few hours, my crazy, like the moon itself, started to wax and wane as Howard doggedly tried to get me to see things differently. My argument up till then had been that there were ten thousand unknown things that could lead to our demise, but Howard's argument was, why not think about the ten thousand things that got us together in the first place?

Oh god, what a stupid thing to say. Does he really think that an effective way to convince me of anything is to just tell me the exact opposite thing? What's next, is he going to tell me it's opposite day? Men are so stooooop—wait, maybe he's onto something. I mean, what if I hadn't gone to that party in New York where I first met Howard's producing partner Emile? What if I hadn't sat next to him on the bus? (The party was on the top of a double-decker tour bus and you had to sit down on the top deck so you wouldn't get clocked by the traffic lights.) What if I didn't want to try television writing? What if Howard never created the television show In Case of Emergency? *What if our first meeting went badly and I didn't get hired? What if Howard hadn't been such a dummy with computers and lost that file on that particular day? What if Howard didn't have a town house with a balcony? What if he had followed the advice of the pros/cons list and decided it was better not to kiss me? What if that first kiss was horrible? What if he didn't call me the very next day after the kiss? What if he didn't convince me that we should secretly start dating even though we worked together? What if my crazy intensity freaked him out? What if he just let me break up with him?*

Later that night, Howard said one of the smartest things I had ever heard when it came to relationships (and not just from a man, but from anyone). He said that in any relationship you care about, you have to "protect the possibility of a happy ending." He then told me it wasn't his original thought, but that he was quoting a famous director of plays, who said that when you direct a romantic comedy you have to find the funny in their arguments and not take things too far into a dark direction because then it could easily turn to a tragedy and—*What is he doing? Is he really schooling me in drama theory right now in the middle of my lame attempt to break up with him? What an absurd situation this is.*

Crazy, as it turns out, listens to stupid better than it listens to smart.

See, crazy and stupid are perfectly matched, and it's not subtle in the least bit but wonderfully and simply obvious. The obvious is called the obvious for one reason only: It's true. You have to be a crazy woman to deal with a stupid man, and you have to be a stupid man to put up with a crazy woman. So maybe it's not quite so complicated as we think it is.

I am hereby proposing a new paradigm—a simple new truth—which is, instead of thinking that the crazy and stupid are what's keeping men and women in conflict with one another, we should pull a Howard and just flip the whole idea on its head and ask ourselves: **What if it's the crazy and the stupid that are keeping us together?**

Howard sometimes says he just wants peace. He says this to me on my craziest days, but I now know him well enough to know that is not what he really wants (he just wants me to stop talking and let him read his newspaper). He's just too stupid to articulate it accurately. I find this incredibly endearing and sweet. Sometimes I think Howard is so totally clueless and he wouldn't survive a day without me, but what I really mean to say is that he is totally clueless and wouldn't survive a day without me, and sure he's stupid, but he's my stupid, and what I mean by that is that I wouldn't want to live a day without him. (And, Howard, for the record, just know that if I was ever going to fake my own death for any reason, I promise I would talk to you about it in person first. Because I could text you or e-mail you, but what if you got it late or forgot your iPhone in your car? Or even lost your glasses in the sand?)

Here is my pros/cons list of being with a stupid man:

Pros: I love him. He loves me. I love him.

Cons: What? Who, me? Why would you think I'd have cons? I'm obviously not the type to think negatively.

AFTERWARD
H AND J

"So . . ."

"So . . . ?"

"So we did it! We just finished writing the whole book and we didn't break up. I guess all your worrying was just you being crazy. And maybe I'm not that stupid after all. And if you're not sure how to act right now, this is the part where you agree."

"The day is still young."

"What?"

"We can still break up. Today."

"We're going to break up today?!"

"You have no idea how far a woman will go to be right. But we can get back together next week. Hey, maybe even tomorrow. What are you doing about three?"

"Oh my god, you are so crazy."

"Where are you going?"

"We're broken up, I can go wherever I want."

"We're not broken up until I say we're broken up. In fact, we've already broken up, we're back together, I was right, you're still stupid, I have cake, you want cake?"

"Well, I love cake . . ."

244

ACKNOWLEDGMENTS

HOWARD: I'd like to thank all the enthusiastic early believers in this book: Sean Malone, who told me to get out of his car and start writing it already, Jonah Nolan and Lisa Joy, Heather Holst, May Chan, Flavio D'Oliveira, Victoria Grantham, Justin Yoffe, Rob Lotterstein, Alan Blanc, Roz Moore, David Holden, and nothing I write is ever complete without a shout out to Sherman. I also have to thank Emile Levisetti, who introduced me to Jenny (and was an early believer, too); Jonathan Silverman and Jennifer Finnigan, whose great romance caused the fight that inspired this book; Heather Maltby, our assistant and Newlywed Game M.C.; Josann McGibbon and Sara Parriot, who told me the secret that "Women are made up of many, many tiny parts"; and the director Jerry Zaks, who *actually* said, "Protect the possibility of a happy ending."

An extra special thanks to Elliot Webb, because he puts up with my kvetching and often matches me kvetch for kvetch; and George Sheanshang, because he's the greatest friend and reader any writer could hope to have.

And to Dustin, who shows me all the things left to write about.

And of course, Jenny Lee, because every day with her is an adventure, and every night is like being at the best slumber party ever.

JENNY: This book would not be possible without the love, encouragement, and support of the following people: my sister-in-law Susan Stonehouse Lee, my nephew Benjamin, and my niece Addison Lee, Doozy, Wendell, Nadine Morrow (and Finn too—you two really kept me sane during the whole process!), the super-helpful Victoria Grantham, Stephanie Staal, Tasha Blaine, Christine Zander, Jessi Klein, Laura Clement, Linda Lazo, Jenner Sullivan, Anne King, Danielle Sacks, Janet Lee, Christina Ohly Evans, Jason Anthony, Caitlin McGinty, Dorian Howard, Ali Isaacs, Kelly Edwards, Richard Russell, Tracy Poust, Ingrid Sheaffer, David Feeney, Lia Langworthy, Ashley Cramer, Heather Maltby, Lisa Joy and Jonah Nolan, Carrie Jacobsen (and The Pilates Place), The Brentwood Art Center, and all the couples who participated in the Newlywed Game, plus Bryan Huddleston, my first boyfriend, and all the other boyfriends and random dates through the years (without your collective stupidity, I could never be this crazy smart about men—ha-ha).

I would also like to give an extra shout out to Howard (which is bizarre, I know, since I wrote this book with him), but he was a true believer in the book well before I was (in my defense, I really and truly thought it would break us up). Without his gentle art of persuasion (the tough love noodging approach), I may have just been crazy enough to let this awesome project pass me by. You're the best boyfriend ever.

HOWARD AND JENNY: We would like to thank our ICM book agent, Andy Barzvi, who believed in this book from the second we walked into her office; all the people at Simon Spotlight Entertainment, and especially, Patrick Price (or as we like to call him Patrick Priceless), our absolutely fabulous editor and most dedicated supporter. We're so freakin' thankful we found you. We couldn't have done it without you.

ABOUT THE AUTHORS

HOWARD J. MORRIS began his career in television, writing for the revolutionary HBO series *Dream On,* and then on the Emmy-nominated *Home Improvement.* He created the series *Holding the Baby* and *In Case of Emergency.* He's also written on *My Wife and Kids, According to Jim,* and most recently, *The Starter Wife.*

JENNY LEE was a writer on the hit comedy series *Samantha Who?,* starring Christina Applegate, and a writer on the Nickelodeon show *The Troop.* She is also the author of three books of humor essays: *Skinny Bitching, What Wendell Wants,* and *I Do. I Did. Now What?!: Life After the Wedding Dress.* She lives with Howard in Los Angeles.